"Unflinching in his analysis, David Gushee traces the sobering history of Christianity's all too frequent complicity in authoritarian rule. Yet Gushee also shows how Christians have within their faith the tools to restore democracy at this critical juncture. Reminding readers that democracy must be fought for, Gushee equips the American church for this battle. *Defending Democracy from Its Christian Enemies* is an immensely important book for our present moment."

—Kristin Kobes Du Mez,
author of *Jesus and John Wayne:
How White Evangelicals Corrupted a Faith and Fractured a Nation*

"David Gushee has done it again, providing clarity, calling, and comfort. The increased risk of the dangers of Christian nationalism is evident from the violent insurrection on January 6 to hostile takeovers of school boards to splits in churches. What is needed is an understanding of the attraction of Christian nationalism and a faithful call forward for those who want to engage a more faithful Christian witness. This book provides just what is needed. The struggle against Christian nationalism has been part of the United States since its founding. And that struggle is ours today. I am so grateful to have David Gushee in the mix and helping to lead the way."

—Doug Pagitt,
executive director of Vote Common Good

"David Gushee has written that rare book that combines reader-friendliness, moral clarity, and political detail. A stellar accomplishment much needed today. Gushee sets America's sociopolitical rifts in context and guides the reader to big-picture thinking about what's at stake in the world today, and he does it in a way that is both elegant and heartfelt. Read it and give it to everyone you know. "

—Marcia Pally,
author of *White Evangelicals and Right-Wing Populism:
How Did We Get Here?*

"Against a bewildering explosion of recent books struggling to make sense of the role of religion in the resurgence of right-wing authoritarian global politics, David Gushee enters the current fray with a signal contribution in *Defending Democracy from Its Christian Enemies*. Not only does he do a marvelous job of documenting the history and current state of global Christian illiberal impulses and tendencies, but he also skillfully explains its most recent incarnation in US politics in the person of President Donald Trump. Not content to merely analyze authoritarian reactionary Christianity, as he calls it, he offers a theological antidote to rising antidemocratic politics in American churches by drawing on the Baptist democratic tradition as well as the Black Christian tradition in the

United States. This is a must read for anyone concerned about the current Christian threats to democracy dominating our headlines."

—Shaun Casey,
author of *Chasing the Devil at Foggy Bottom:
The Future of Religion in American Diplomacy*

"David Gushee investigates key historical and current moments in which Christians have served as zealous guardians of reactionary political programs and authoritarian regimes. His book draws on sound biblical and theological resources to offer a timely, eloquent, and compelling apologetic for democracy. *Defending Democracy* deserves the close attention of ethically minded Christians during this time of political turbulence and moral confusion!"

—Hak Joon Lee, Fuller Theological Seminary

"The most persistent myth in US history is the notion that we are a Christian nation. Without denigrating the contributions of the Christian religion to the development of American society, David Gushee critiques idolatrous forms of authoritarian reactionary Christianity that actively undermine democratic institutions, which in his analysis reflects a global trend toward populist antidemocratic politics. In place of religious totalitarianism Gushee offers a Christian defense of democracy, applicable *mutatis mutandis* in other political and religious contexts, that aims to restore the American idea once eloquently described by Alexis de Toqueville as a 'beacon on a hill.'"

—Rubén Rosario Rodríguez, Saint Louis University

"This is an important book. It asks about the ways in which Christians may favor autocratic politics over democracy and does not shy away from difficulties. It analyses how authoritarian regimes can legitimate their power by playing into religious sentiments. Thus, it gives a theological foundation to the need for political awareness within Christian circles. Its analysis should be read by theologians, Christians in general, and all those who are politically engaged."

—Bert Jan Lietaert Peerbolte, Vrije Universiteit Amsterdam

"The bonds between Christianity and democracy are frayed as never before, not only in the United States but around the globe. In *Defending Democracy from Its Christian Enemies*, one of our best Christian ethicists takes on this crucial topic and charts a way forward—one that does not entail obeisance to a 'Christian strongman.' This is a very good and important book."

—Randall Balmer, author of
Bad Faith: Race and the Rise of the Religious Right

DEFENDING DEMOCRACY FROM ITS CHRISTIAN ENEMIES

David P. Gushee

WILLIAM B. EERDMANS PUBLISHING COMPANY
GRAND RAPIDS, MICHIGAN

Wm. B. Eerdmans Publishing Co.
4035 Park East Court SE, Grand Rapids, Michigan 49546
www.eerdmans.com

© 2023 David P. Gushee
Published 2023
Printed in the United States of America

29 28 27 26 25 24 23   1 2 3 4 5 6 7

ISBN 978-0-8028-8293-6

Library of Congress Cataloging-in-Publication Data

A catalog record for this book is available from the Library of
Congress.

For all who have sacrificed to defend democracy

Contents

Acknowledgments

I begin by thanking Anita Eerdmans, president and publisher of Eerdmans Publishing Company, and James Ernest, vice president and editor-in-chief, for the privilege of writing this book for them. James Ernest first suggested the concept, and the entire Eerdmans staff has displayed its customary excellence at every step. Eerdmans folks, I will never forget our dinner together in Grand Rapids in 2021, talking it all over. There was hope that night!

I also thank my agent David Morris of Hyponymous Consulting, who was part of that dinner and has helped in so many ways to make this book a reality.

The kernel of this project was first presented in May 2022 as my inaugural address as Chair in Christian Social Ethics for the Faculty of Religion and Theology at Vrije Universiteit (VU-FRT) Amsterdam. Shortly thereafter, the work benefited immensely from a detailed discussion in the Peace, Trauma, and Religion Working Group of VU-FRT.

I am also grateful to the good folks of First Baptist Church, Winston-Salem, North Carolina, for being the first American audience to engage with this material, during my visit in August 2022.

In Fall 2022, the leaders of the European Baptist theological seminaries devoted their attention to the ideas discussed in this book. I also presented US-related material to the Christianity and Democracy Today conference at Tübingen University in late October 2022. I am grateful especially to Paul Peterson of Tübingen for that invitation and much rich dialogue.

My goal in this work is a discussion relevant to the US setting but also far beyond. These gatherings have been an important part of any progress I have made toward speaking cogently into these different settings. While the book inevitably reflects the US context that I know so well and in which I am daily immersed, my fond hope is that it will have succeeded in drawing global connections and speaking beyond our shores.

I thank my advance readers: Wayne Anderson, Henk Bakker, Jacob Cook, Lynnie Grant, Dirk-Martin Grube, Jon Huckins, Andre Lisboa, David Morris, Marcia Pally, Mike Pears, Bert Jan Lietaert Peerbolte, Paul Peterson, Ron Sanders, Isaac Sharp, Richard Weaver, Erica Whitaker, Reggie Williams, and Ken Wilson. This book is much stronger because of your insights, and I am deeply grateful.

I offer special thanks to my dear wife, Jeanie, always my best and most careful reader, the only person who endured both my first draft and every draft till the end. Jeanie constantly challenges me to think beyond the categories of one side of the left/right binary. How indispensable her voice is in making me be a more rigorous and fair-minded thinker.

Three members of a prior generation helped shape the deep commitment to democracy that informs this project. All were devout Christians. Two were committed Republicans, one an equally committed Democrat.

My late father, David E. Gushee, served the Congressional Research Service of the United States Congress as an energy and environment policy analyst. I learned at his feet the value of a merit-based professional civil service informing effective democratic policymaking. He was also a combat veteran who served with bravery in the US Army during the Korean War. My father-in-law, W. Vance Grant Jr., a Navy veteran who served in the Pacific during World War II, also worked in the US civil service for many decades, primarily the Department of Education. These men were Christians who loved their country, loved democracy, and loved government service. My primary mentor, the late Glen Stassen, receives significant scholarly engagement in this volume. Glen also loved democracy, to his core. He believed in a democratic, Baptist, Christian, activist vision and practice. His thought will be engaged seriously here.

This book is so very much better because of the example and input of all these I have named. Of course, as always, all responsibility for the errors or weaknesses of this book belongs to me.

Eerdmans wanted a brief book, something like a manifesto. The final product is not as brief as they wanted, as I believed it necessary to engage various subjects in more depth than anticipated. But, in keeping with their wishes, the style of this book mainly takes the form of concise essays reflecting closely on a handful of key resources about each subject. My heartfelt gratitude is offered to the authors, living and dead, of the key works deployed.

I have sought, as I usually do, to write a book both accessible to a broad audience and engaging for scholars. Two ways I have tried to do that are to avoid or clearly define technical language, and to use punchy subheadings. For the latter, I thank Ken Wilson for his special help.

Much of my recent publishing has drawn heavily on my own journey into and out of US evangelicalism. In this book, by contrast, I will offer relatively few references to myself or my experiences. This book is about democracy, not about me.

Still, thirty years of serving mainly in the United States and some in the global evangelical subculture, as well as considerable engagement with US policy debates and policymakers, has left me some indelibly instructive experiences, some of which will be shared here.

This book arose initially from my shock, horror, and heartbreak over radical threats to democracy in my country, feelings shared by millions of us here in the United States. We have seen things we could not have imagined—blood spilled in the US Capitol building (of all places), in an insurrection partially led by self-identified

Christians (of all people), threats to democracy in the news each day even now. This extraordinary crisis is the reason this book jumped the line over other projects and is now in the world.

A final comment about time, and timing. This manuscript was finalized on December 1, 2022. But history rumbles on. Especially the chapters about recent events in several countries will suffer from the passage of time. All of us will need to keep reading, and learning, and deciding what is required of us, as crucial events unfold in the days to come.

David P. Gushee
Atlanta, Georgia, USA

Introduction

This book does not intend to say everything that could be said about the relationship between Christianity and democracy, but it does intend to say four important things:

1. Christians should support democracy because, despite its many imperfections, it is the best political system yet developed.
2. Many Christians, in the United States and around the world, instead favor or are open to authoritarian and reactionary political trends that pose a grave threat to open and free democracy.
3. Due to this tendency, Christians turn out to be among the leading threats to democracy in much of the world, and this is not at all where Christians should be located politically.
4. Responsible Christians need to recommit to democracy, with Christian leaders guiding the Christian community toward a defense and practice of democracy that fit with the convictions of Christian ethics.

This book is intended to be descriptive, diagnostic, and normative. That means:

1. It will offer descriptive accounts of relevant Christian political movements and historical moments in different countries, mainly involving examples of Christians drifting into authoritarianism and reactionary politics that undercut democracy.
2. It will offer a diagnosis of why many Christians are tempted

toward or explicitly prefer authoritarian reactionary politics to democracy as part of their negative reaction to modern cultural developments.

3. It will offer an argument for today's Christians to support a particular vision of democratic politics, and traditional Christian resources to undergird that vision.

No claim is offered in this book that only nominal, brainwashed, or apostate Christians support authoritarian rule, while all serious, devout, and faithful Christians support democracy. This kind of claim would be neither fair nor true. There are serious reasons for Christians to be skeptical of democracy, in theory and in current practice, and to be attracted to what I will shorthand as authoritarian reactionary Christian politics. Certainly, such political views have not been rare in history or among Christians today. The reasons for such antidemocratic political leanings need to be thoroughly examined if one wants to understand them and create conditions for healthier Christian politics.

Of course, there indeed have been times when Christians (or "Christians") have leaned into antidemocratic politics based on an apostate, heretical, and immoralist version of Christianity. This is occurring today as it has in the past. We will encounter and repudiate some of these in this book.

As an American, I acknowledge that this book is a reflection on the era associated with former president Donald Trump—especially with the shocking events after the November 2020 election, when avowed Christians, acting for explicitly Christian reasons, were at the forefront of those who sought to prevent the certification of Joe Biden as the forty-sixth US president. Their dangerous attitudes were seen most strongly in those who violently breached the US Capitol building on January 6, 2021.

More broadly, it is a reflection on the obvious phenomenon of Christian political radicalization in the United States. This radicalization, and the startling threat that it continues to pose to democracy in the United States, remains the main story in American politics today. All Christians need to understand it and respond to it.

Our current moment in the United States represents a profoundly troubling existential crisis for many of us who once took the functioning of American democracy for granted. We find ourselves fearful, alarmed, and disoriented. We have experienced psychological distress, frayed family bonds, divided churches, intimidated pastors, and destroyed friendships, all because of politics. We have not been here before. And so we ask: *What happened to our country? What went wrong with our religion? Why didn't we see this coming?* When we are disoriented, we need clear understanding to move to purposeful action. This is what scholars are supposed to offer. Every word written here is for these purposes.

In the process of undertaking what began as a US-focused inquiry, I learned that our US crisis is related to a broader crisis. Explicitly Christian antidemocratic political movements are quite visible around the world today—and have also been a significant historical reality. We will touch down on a number of these situations in the pages to come, as we consider case studies from France, Germany, Russia, Poland, Hungary, and Brazil, as well as the United States. Other historical and current examples were readily available.

While each national story is different, the similarity—and in some cases, actual interconnections—between antidemocratic Christian politics and leaders in different historically "Christian" countries proves to be deeply instructive. This crisis of democracy is far more than merely a US trend. Despite national differences, the characteristics of what I will call authoritarian reactionary Christian politics are widely shared. This is a global phenomenon. Read widely enough and you find the same notes struck—on the left and the right and the befuddled center—all over the world.

It is interesting to note that the religiously authoritarian antidemocratic trend extends beyond the Christian world. Contemporary Turkey under Prime Minister Recep Tayyip Erdoğan offers an example from the Muslim-majority world, while India under Prime Minister Narendra Modi offers one from the Hindu-majority world. I do not address these developments because I believe they are best left to specialists in those religious and national traditions. Their apparent similarities to the historically Christian countries, however, are fascinating. Perhaps the analytical model I will develop here will prove helpful to other religious traditions.

This book has been written in 2022 for publication in 2023. It was first aimed toward the specific practical goal that US Christians be equipped to not do further harm to democracy in our nation during the 2024 election cycle. That hope I now extend to all other countries considered here, and indeed everywhere democracy is threatened and Christians are part of the problem.

This is a book in Christian ethics, which aims to form Christians to be faithful followers of Jesus Christ. One perennial and very challenging aspect of Christian ethics is political ethics—how Christians should engage government, the state, and politics. In my experience, this is an area in which Christians are generally instructed very poorly by their pastors—if they are instructed at all.

While I am not attempting to offer a systematic and comprehensive Christian political theology, I *am* attempting the narrower project of offering a warning and a vision for Christians in societies that have democracy but are at risk of losing it, in part because of Christian temptations to authoritarianism arising in response to panic over liberalizing cultural trends. In sketching aspects of a moral vision for the contemporary Christian defense of democracy, I will retrieve three elements of historic Christian political thought and practice that I think are especially helpful: the Baptist democratic tradition, the Black Christian democratic tradition, and covenantal Christian political ethics. I hope this is a start, at least.

Fundamentally, then, like all works in Christian ethics, this is a book intended to shape the moral vision and practice of Christian people. But I hope that this book may also prove interesting to anyone who cares about a difficult dynamic in the political life of many societies filled with large numbers of traditionalist Christians. That is much of the world. They (we) have repeatedly proven susceptible to authoritarian reactionary Christian politics, even at the cost of weakening or destroying democracy. Those who want to understand and counteract this problem might find some help here.

This book is written by a US American Christian democrat. I am a Christian first and always, a Baptist minister who also attends Catholic services with my wife. I also dearly love my country, and I am ardently committed to strengthening its democracy for the sake of future generations, including my own grandchildren.

In my professional circles, I have become fairly well known, and sometimes quickly written off, as a man of the left. This is unfortunate. I would rather be understood as a committed Christian, called to pastoral and scholarly ministry, whose political ideology leans center-left in the US democratic context—and who has arrived at that ideology not via MSNBC but *through my reading of the biblical prophetic tradition and the teachings of Jesus.* Beyond my congregational and denominational identity, I now feel at home in the growing *post-evangelical* Christian community, millions strong, filled with people of similar convictions.[1]

As I survey the bitter division between left and right in the United States and much of the world, I believe that public debate in our countries desperately needs the contribution of people whose commitments are not easily pigeonholed as "secular left" or "religious right" and who can offer needed challenge and affirmation to both sides. At a theological-ethical level, we need *mediating voices*

1. The most relevant of my books for those who are interested in understanding my convictions are the following: David P. Gushee and Glen H. Stassen, *Kingdom Ethics: Following Jesus in Contemporary Context*, 2nd ed. (Grand Rapids: Eerdmans, 2016); David P. Gushee, *Changing Our Mind*, 3rd ed. (Canton, MI: Read the Spirit Books, 2019); David P. Gushee, *Still Christian: Following Jesus Out of American Evangelicalism* (Louisville: Westminster John Knox, 2017); David P. Gushee, *After Evangelicalism: The Path to a New Christianity* (Louisville: Westminster John Knox, 2020).

who are seriously committed to Christian faith and morality, willing to engage respectfully the world we live in today, and able to speak to starkly different types of people—including those holding mutually incomprehensible versions of Christian faith. I hope that is what I offer here.

I do believe that the greatest threat to democracy today comes from the right, mainly but not exclusively the religious right. The bulk of this book will offer the argument reflected by my title: *democracy needs to be defended from its Christian enemies.* How we got here, and what we do about it, is the subject of the reflections that follow.

1

Defining and Defending Democracy

> Man's capacity for justice makes democracy possible,
> but man's inclination to injustice makes democracy
> necessary. In all non-democratic political theories
> the state or the ruler is invested with uncontrolled
> power for the sake of achieving order and unity in
> the community. But the pessimism which prompts
> and justifies this policy is not consistent; for it is not
> applied, as it should be, to the ruler.
>
> —Reinhold Niebuhr (1944)[1]

This is a book about the relationship between Christianity and democracy. Before going further, we need to try to define what we mean by that weighty word "democracy." It is not at all simple. There is not agreement in the popular or scholarly literature about how to define the term, or whether it is accurate to describe countries like the United States as actually being democracies, or whether democracy should be the aspiration of the people who live within these countries.

This itself is highly disorienting. It will be our first important discovery as we try to make sense of today's political chaos: the supposedly "democratic" political systems that some of us took for

---

1. Reinhold Niebuhr, *The Children of Light and the Children of Darkness* (New York: Scribner's, 1944), xiii.

7

granted are conceptually messier than we knew. And here is the second discovery: In some of our countries, internal social and political divisions may be exposing and worsening that conceptual messiness and testing every bulwark of political stability that we once thought was solid and substantial.

Democracy as Rule of the People without Rule of the Mob

One must begin somewhere. So, just to pick a place, we begin with the thumbnail definition of democracy offered by Yale University political scientist Bruce Russert, who says that a democracy is a political system "in which nearly everyone can vote, elections are freely contested, the chief executive is chosen by popular vote or by an elected parliament, and civil rights and civil liberties are substantially guaranteed."[2] For Russert, then, a democracy is a political system in which the people choose their leaders and in which the civil rights and freedoms of all are protected by law. This seems a familiar and reasonable starting point.

Political scientist David Koyzis defines the shared characteristics of Western-style democracies more extensively: universal franchise for adult citizens; equal franchise power (every vote is weighted the same); majority rule; competitive elections and the right to stand for public office; freedom of speech and of the press; rights charters aiming to protect core citizen liberties and minority rights; and the rule of law, embodied in a written or unwritten constitution.[3] Koyzis reminds us that the concept of the rule of law long preceded the idea of democracy.[4] Indeed it did, by many centuries; consider

2. Bruce Russert, "Advance Democracy, Human Rights, and Religious Liberty," in *Just Peacemaking: Ten Practices for Abolishing War*, ed. Glen H. Stassen (Cleveland: Pilgrim Press, 1998), 96.

3. David T. Koyzis, *Political Visions and Illusions: A Survey and Critique of Contemporary Ideologies* (Downers Grove, IL: InterVarsity Press, 2003), 126.

4. Koyzis, *Political Visions and Illusions*, 129.

the eighteenth-century BCE Babylonian Code of Hammurabi. But, of course, this was law as dictated by an absolute monarch. It is *when rule of law and democracy are put together* that we get into the neighborhood of modern democracy, which both aims to reflect the will of the majority (popular sovereignty) and to set limits on the majority's powers through constitutionally based legal structures (rule of law).

In a democracy, the people or their representatives write the constitution and make the laws, so the principle of popular sovereignty is protected, and even the rule of law appears to be subsumed under popular sovereignty. But, on the other hand, wise constitution-drafters recognize that irresponsible or impulsive exercises of popular sovereignty must be constrained; this is why the constitutions and the fundamental laws of most democracies are crafted so that they are very difficult to amend.

Legal theory has discovered and frequently explores a profound paradox in relation to democratic lawmaking: in a democracy, law is made by the people, but it somehow must reflect transcendent principles that go beyond merely popular will. Conservative Harvard Law School professor Adrian Vermeule has recently argued, in a powerful (though in some ways alarming) treatment of US constitutional law, that in the classical legal tradition law is not viewed merely as the product of the legislator or the popular will.[5] Law gains its moral legitimacy insofar as it reflects principles of the natural law (*ius naturale*) that both transcend and ground civil laws.

Natural law is essentially transcendent, objective, universal moral truth. In Catholic natural law thinking, the natural law is understood to reflect God's moral will and to be accessible to human beings through their God-given reason, which has been damaged but not ruined by human sin. Reason survives sufficiently to dis-

---

5. Adrian Vermeule, *Common Good Constitutionalism* (Cambridge: Polity Press, 2022). What is alarming is that Vermeule explicitly relativizes the significance of democratic governance vis-à-vis governance that advances the common good. This has certain implications. More on this issue later.

cern natural law and to conform the human will to its principles. Natural law thinking can be and has been secularized in modern times to strip out reference to God but to retain the rest of the theory: there is rationally discernible moral structure to the universe, this grounds human moral obligation, and laws should correspond within their proper purview.

Vermeule argues that the core natural law principle related to government is that the fundamental purpose of political authority is to advance the common good of the community. He draws on ancient thought to define the common good as "the highest felicity or happiness of the whole political community," or specifically as "peace, justice, and abundance."[6] Rulers' actions, including lawmaking, that advance the common good fit with the natural law. Not everyone accepts the concept of natural law, but even if one does not, it should be clear that for laws to be received as legitimate in a democracy, the vast majority of the citizenry must agree that they are reasonable and just. Otherwise, law is merely an expression of raw power.

We will return to this difficult conversation about natural law at various times in this book, for it is an important part of the current debate over democracy. For now, let us simply say that democracy consists of popular sovereignty through the rule of laws that are not arbitrary but grounded in moral principles that the people themselves respect.

In a democracy, people rule themselves, directly ("direct democracy") or through elected representatives ("representative democracy") who make laws that govern the community. Political communities and democratic political associations such as clubs and sports leagues seem normally to develop in something like this order: a group of people first create (or recognize) the existence of themselves as a "polity" (a human group or community) that wants

6. Vermeule, *Common Good Constitutionalism*, 7.

to gather for a shared purpose. Then they agree together to develop the polity's initial governance structure, either as a committee of the whole or through representatives. This usually involves establishing a constitution, then writing at first basic and eventually more elaborate rules/laws, and finally developing sturdy processes for that community's ongoing management and continued vitality. This latter task includes maintaining agreed procedures for determining the best interests and will of the community, revising the rules/laws, periodically selecting new leaders, and protecting the interests and rights of all who are members. This, I argue, is the core of democratic self-government. Note that patterns of human voluntary association at a grassroots level precede the development of larger-scale political communities but require (and develop) similar skills. We will discuss this matter more thoroughly later in this book.

Note that democracy as defined here already carries far more meaning than simply "rule of the people," its Greek etymological derivation. It was discovered as early as the first Greek experiment in democracy 2,500 years ago that "rule of the people" alone is not sufficient as a governance philosophy, for several reasons: the problem of the tyranny of a majority over various kinds of minorities, the ability of sophisticated but amoral rhetoricians ("sophists") to sway the emotions of the people in unconstructive and irrational ways, the unwieldiness of mass-group decision-making processes in a community of any size, the possibility of a descent into bitterly conflicted factions who hate each other more than they care about the well-being of the community, the lack of readiness of many ordinary people to exercise the informed and wise judgment necessary for democratic self-government, and the instability of a political community not governed by some fixed basic laws. An effective democracy looks like the wise self-rule of a people without the collapse into mob tyranny, faction, irrationality, or self-destruction.

Does My Liberal Democracy Look Too Thin?

Democracy is not just a theory but a long human experiment in community building that by now has solidified into a democratic tradition.[7] In Western culture, democratic theorizing and tradition began in ancient Greece. But modern democratic theory making and governance are generally traced to stirrings in medieval Christian Europe (such as Iceland's parliament, created in 930, and the Magna Carta in England in 1215), and then the quickening of a serious democratization movement beginning in the seventeenth and eighteenth centuries, with breakthrough developments occurring in the democratic revolutions in France and the United States in the late eighteenth century.

The most important, or at least most remembered, democratic theorizing in the formative early modern period of the late seventeenth century was offered by English philosopher John Locke (1632–1704). Locke's contribution to democratic theory was deeply affected by the bloody political conflicts in his nation, which included violence, revolution, and counterrevolution in the name of competing versions of state Christianity.[8]

In this context, Locke developed the core elements of what became known as liberal democratic theory. His approach was essentially individualist, libertarian, and negative. Locke imagined government as emerging from the self-interested decision of free individuals (implicitly: landed, wealthy, educated males) agreeing to form governments powerful enough to protect each individual's

7. For democracy as an "experiment," I am indebted to Robert Garland, in his Great Courses treatment of "Athenian Democracy: An Experiment for the Ages" (Chantilly, VA: The Teaching Company, 2018). For democracy as a tradition, see Jeffrey Stout, *Democracy and Tradition* (Princeton: Princeton University Press, 2004).

8. The most important work is his "Two Treatises of Government" (1690). See John Locke, *Two Treatises of Government*, ed. Peter Laslett (New York: New American Library, 1960).

security, freedom, privacy, and personal pursuit of happiness but uninterested in advancing a substantive shared vision of what is true, right, and good. The latter project had over centuries led to religious coercion and civil strife. Liberal democracy would limit government's role and maximize individual liberty of conscience and action.

This formative early vision is sometimes described as creating a "thin," "liberal," or "libertarian" democratic tradition. Its strength was its realistic recognition of the reality of convictional pluralism and the dangers of government meddling in matters of conscience so important to people that they will fight and die for their beliefs. Its weaknesses, however, were at least twofold. Its social imagination focused on individuals and their personal preferences rather than communities and their shared needs—but it is really communities that build associations and ultimately national governments. Further, its realism did not extend to recognizing that some shared account of the good life and the good community, and some way of forming good citizens who can exercise responsible freedom, is required to sustain a viable human community—even a political community. Liberal democracy has been described as a "thin" tradition because of these omissions.

An instructive project for any reader might be to pick up the US Declaration of Independence and Constitution and read these in their entirety. These hugely influential documents offer relatively little by way of a shared communal vision. The Declaration mainly protests the depredations of British rule and demands political independence based on the fundamental created equality of "all men" and their "unalienable rights" to "life, liberty, and the pursuit of happiness." While much has been made of this language, in context the main point appears to be that colonists laboring under the British yoke "were entitled to exercise the same rights of self-government as other peoples."[9]

---

9. Quoting from Stanford historian Jack N. Rakove. See his "What Remains of Thomas Jefferson?" *Wall Street Journal*, July 2-3, 2022, C1-2.

The US Constitution's Preamble does a bit more, claiming that
it is written "in order to form a more perfect union, establish justice, insure domestic tranquility, provide for the common defence,
promote the general welfare, and secure the blessings of liberty for
ourselves and our posterity." After that, it focuses on setting up
rather detailed governance structures. The Bill of Rights (the first
ten amendments to the Constitution), added four years later under
the pressure of the ratification debate, mainly protects a list of specific individual freedoms from government overreach, in a classic
libertarian move. No effort is made in the Constitution to specify
a substantive vision of "justice" or of "the general welfare."[10] It can
be argued that this substantive vision was assumed, or that it was
purposefully omitted. Either way, later generations have had to deal
with its absence.

10. In the United States, the Constitution has been treated as nearly
sacred. Vermeule shows how conservatives have attempted to treat it like
sacred Scripture through a reading theory called "originalism" that he
(Vermeule) absolutely dismantles in his *Common Good Constitutionalism*
(ch. 3). But in his substantively conservative way he also attacks a liberal
"progressive constitutionalism," which in his view simply allows judges
to read their liberationist project into the Constitution to arrive at decisions like the 2015 *Obergefell* ruling legalizing gay marriage (ch. 4). Meanwhile, law professors Ryan D. Doerfler and Samuel Moyn recently posted
a startling op-ed in the *New York Times* arguing that the US constitution is
"broken" and that we need to "reclaim America from constitutionalism."
Doerfler and Moyn, "Liberals Need to Change the Rules," *New York Times*,
August 21, 2022, 9. Both sides, left and right, all brilliant legal scholars,
appear to agree that the Constitution, and the judiciary constantly called
upon to interpret it, cannot bear the weight that American society, politics,
and law are asking it to bear. That may be because its substantive moral
vision is simply inadequate. It may also be because our society's substantive moral conflicts are too grave for a (morally thin) eighteenth-century
constitution to adjudicate.

Even a Democracy Needs Moral Virtues, Values, and Vision

It is highly doubtful whether human communities can function without any kind of shared values or a vision of what a good life and good community look like. Even the relatively minimalist kinds of goals that are articulated in liberal democratic constitutional documents, like advancing the general welfare, would benefit from a shared understanding of what that might look like. But no such substantive vision is on offer, because the individualist-libertarian vision prevails, quite intentionally. There is no collective common good; there is only the aggregation of individual goods as we each pursue our own version of happiness.[11]

As we will discuss in chapter 12, it helped quite a bit that in the societies within which early democracies developed, the religious loyalties of the people were predominantly Christian. Many of the very earliest democratic writings in the Western world—decades before Locke—were offered in much "thicker" and morally substantive Christian terms. And some of the very earliest experiments in democratic polity-building were undertaken in dissenting "free churches," almost two hundred years before the late eighteenth-century democratic political revolutions. (The minority Jewish communities in this period also had distinct moral traditions, especially sharpened by their very difficult experience as a religious minority in discriminatory Christian lands. These traditions formed the values and vision of Jewish citizens—when they were allowed to be citizens—and shaped their support for the essential principles of early modern democracy.) This religious, moral, and political background filled in much of the moral substance that was intentionally left out of liberal democratic constitutional documents.

---

11. Vermeule, in *Common Good Constitutionalism* (26), argues that this all-too-common understanding of "the common good" is actually an antonym for the common good and has no basis in classical politics and legal theory.

The *kinds of people* required to operate these new democratic systems—to govern well, to vote wisely, to debate civilly, to write good laws, to live with minimal state supervision—were produced by already-existing moral communities that inculcated moral virtues, values, and vision. Christian ethicist Ron Sanders puts it this way: "Democracy is a 'thin' tradition, because it rests on a negative ethic of non-interference and avoiding harm to the liberty of others. It needs a complementary tradition with the virtues to carry it forward. That is why it has flourished in the West, because a thick Christianity has those virtues."[12]

But what happens when democratic societies from the formerly Christian world lose that thick Christian (and Jewish) tradition once central to their populations? Are our liberal democracies today too "thin," or too morally conflicted, to survive?

A Scale to Measure Democratic Health

And yet democracy continues. Billions of people live within democratic countries. Democratic political leaders, activist groups, and scholars continue the effort to strengthen democracy, even as its underpinnings seem shaky in many lands.

Freedom House (FH), the highly respected global pro-democracy organization, will be a significant source in this book.[13] The list of criteria that they use in evaluating the democratic health of every country is congenial to my approach, and I applaud them for their strenuous advocacy for democracy. The basic categories they probe are political rights and civil liberties. The twenty-four evaluative questions they ask in relation to these categories are as follows:

12. Ron Sanders, via private communication with the author. See also Ron Scott Sanders and Scotty McLennan, *After the Election: Prophetic Politics in a Post-Secular Age* (Eugene, OR: Wipf & Stock, 2018).

13. See https://tinyurl.com/yj83mtnx.

Political Rights

- Was the current head of government or other chief national authority elected through free and fair elections?
- Were the current national legislative representatives elected through free and fair elections?
- Are the electoral laws and framework fair, and are they implemented impartially by the relevant election management bodies?
- Do the people have the right to organize in different political parties or other competitive political groupings of their choice, and is the system free of undue obstacles to the rise and fall of these competing parties or groupings?
- Is there a realistic opportunity for the opposition to increase its support or gain power through elections?
- Are the people's political choices free from domination by forces that are external to the political sphere, or by political forces that employ extrapolitical means?
- Do various segments of the population (including ethnic, racial, religious, gender, LGBTQ+, and other relevant groups) have full political rights and electoral opportunities?
- Do the freely elected head of government and national legislative representatives determine the policies of the government?
- Are safeguards against official corruption strong and effective?
- Does the government operate with openness and transparency?

Civil Liberties

- Are there free and independent media?
- Are individuals free to practice and express their religious faith or nonbelief in public and private?
- Is there academic freedom, and is the educational system free from extensive political indoctrination?
- Are individuals free to express their personal views on polit-

17

ical or other sensitive topics without fear of surveillance or
retribution?

- Is there freedom of assembly?
- Is there freedom for nongovernmental organizations, partic-
ularly those that are engaged in human rights–related and
governance-related work?
- Is there freedom for trade unions and similar professional or
labor organizations?
- Is there an independent judiciary?
- Does due process prevail in civil and criminal matters?
- Is there protection from the illegitimate use of physical force
and freedom from war and insurgencies?
- Do laws, policies, and practices guarantee equal treatment of
various segments of the population?
- Do individuals enjoy freedom of movement, including the ability
to change their place of residence, employment, or education?
- Are individuals able to exercise the right to own property and
establish private businesses without undue interference from
state or nonstate actors?
- Do individuals enjoy equality of opportunity and freedom from
economic exploitation?

Democratic Norms and Their Recent Erosion

Now here is another list of democratic norms and best practices
that I have generated, based on hard experience and difficult lessons learned in the United States in recent years. This list is framed
not as questions but as norms and practices requisite to a healthy
democracy:

- Freedom of speech, guaranteed by law, with a diverse media
that is not controlled or intimidated by the government or
anyone else, all part of a culture of vigorous and free public

participation in debate and protest related to public policy and the common good. (I note here that free-speech rights cannot be absolute, and that social media has proven over the last two decades to be a largely unchecked, sometimes antidemocratic force deranged by bad-faith actors and a capitalism without moral scruples.)[14]

· Scrupulous freedom and fairness in every matter involving elections, including the strict political neutrality of election officials, the setting of election dates, voting rules, and vote-counting processes, a culture of respect for the results of elections, and the celebration of a tradition of the peaceful transfer of power on the part of all political parties and candidates.

· A culture in which government officials are focused on the public good rather than private gain, their actions constrained by laws and norms preventing bribery, self-aggrandizement, and corruption; officials are paid adequately but not exorbitantly, operating from a vision of the common good and the intrinsic value of public service.

· The development of a professional civil service hired on merit, insulated from political pressure, and serving across multiple government administrations; while a tiny leadership cadre of political appointees is put in place by the government of the moment, most civil servants stay in their posts through the length of their careers, and even the upper-tier political appointees submit to departmental traditions and best practices.

· Respect for the rule of law, including firm norms and laws against perjury, submission to subpoenas to appear in court, sanctions against frivolous abuse of lawsuits, rigorous and en-

14. For a riveting analysis of the disastrous effects of social media in the United States, see Jonathan Haidt, "After Babel: How Social Media Dissolved the Mortar of Society and Made America Stupid," *Atlantic*, May 2022, 56–66.

forced professional standards for lawyers, and the enforcement of decisions rendered by the courts, regardless of preferences on the part of enforcement agencies, authorities, or individuals.

- Careful constraint and public oversight of the coercion- and violence-wielding institutions of the state, notably the tax authority, police, prisons, and military, and a culture protecting these institutions from political manipulation and unjust deployment.
- Given that nearly every country is constituted by multiple ethnic groups, the enforcement of equal civil rights regardless of ethnic identification or majority status; knowing the power of racial prejudice, government leaders and civil society attend proactively to ensuring fairness for all groups and individuals.
- A culture of serious, virtuous citizenship, with civil-society organizations working to advance democratic norms, deep commitment of citizens to the freedoms and responsibilities of democracy, and a perpetual effort to fight any of the corruption that so commonly ruins governments and nations.

A Few Vulnerabilities of Democracy

As noted above, democracy has always had its critics, and its vulnerabilities are obvious both in theory and in practice. Much of that criticism has been well deserved, though it is also true that these criticisms have been addressed over centuries of refinement in the practices of various democracies.

Here is a reprise of a few of the key worries about democracy, and how they have been addressed as democratic traditions have developed:

- Because democracy can simply become the tyranny of the majority (or, sometimes, a tyranny of a minority when it can capture key mechanisms of governance),[15] healthy democracies develop

15. I credit Marcia Pally for this point about minority capture, via pri-

constitutions with bills of rights, and many other guardrails to protect individual and group rights from being trampled.

· Because democratic decision-making is dangerously vulnerable to the skills of demagogues and the unruly passions and short-term thinking of the moment, healthy democracies develop constitutional structures, deliberative processes, structures for long-range thinking, and cultural dimensions that attack demagoguery, challenge dangerous passions, slow impulsive decision-making, take the long view, and create ways to check or remove tyrants.

· Because democracy, like all political systems, is distorted by unjust concentrations of economic and social power as well as by capitalist practices unchecked by moral scruples or any apparent concern for the common good, healthy democracies undertake constant efforts to redistribute power beyond family and corporate aristocracies, to set appropriate constraints on capitalist economic powers and practices, and to limit the role of money in politics. It is not too much to say that without economic democracy there can be no real political democracy.[16]

vate communication with the author. See also Jamelle Bouie, "Expanding Democracy Is the Solution," *New York Times*, June 5, 2022, 9. Bouie argues that US democracy, at least, has involved the battle of two different "minority" groups – racial, economic, and cultural elites, on the one hand, over against groups of the dispossessed, on the other. In much of US history, powerful elite minorities have behaved in antidemocratic ways in order to disenfranchise relatively powerless minorities, such as Black Americans. This is minority capture of the mechanisms of government.

16. For influential discussions in recent Christian ethics and religious studies, see Luke Bretherton, *Christianity and Contemporary Politics* (Chichester, UK: Wiley-Blackwell, 2010), *Resurrecting Democracy: Faith, Citizenship, and the Politics of a Common Life* (Cambridge: Cambridge University Press, 2015), and *Christ and the Common Life: Political Theology and the Case for Democracy* (Grand Rapids: Eerdmans, 2019); Gary Dorrien, *Soul in Society: The Making and Renewal of Social Christianity* (Minneapolis: Fortress, 1995), and *Social Democracy in the Making: Political and Religious Roots of European Socialism* (New Haven: Yale University Press, 2019); Jeffrey Stout,

- Because democracy is at risk if ill-informed people have no idea what they are doing in the political arena, healthy democracies make every effort to educate their citizenry. They also generally decide that direct democracy should be rare relative to the development of representative systems involving the competitive election of the most qualified and most capable leaders who represent the best of the people.

- Because democracy is messy and contentious, full of arguments and conflicts, healthy democracies find ways to cool conflicts, clarify debates, and seek compromises.

- Because democracy needs a citizenry committed to the democratic tradition and capable of exercising the virtues required to live as free people in community, healthy democracies attend to teaching democratic citizenship and its associated moral values and virtues.

Christianity and Democracy: A Fraught History

The peculiar development of the relationship between religion and politics in Europe and lands colonized by Europeans has added a dimension of Christian antidemocratic critique that in some cases continues today and must still be addressed.

Democracy at its early modern origins reflected an uprising of the bourgeois and eventually lower classes, which challenged, weakened, and/or replaced monarchies and aristocracies that were officially Christian—and that were tied to officially established and culturally dominant Christian churches. Thus, in many lands, the birth of democracy was viewed by some believers as a rebellion against God, God's appointed rulers, the Church, and God's law. This concern is often associated with the term "liberal democracy," and undergirded Christian attacks on democracy for several centuries.

Blessed Are the Organized: Grassroots Democracy in America (Princeton: Princeton University Press, 2012).

Christian democrats have had to show—repeatedly—why democracy is compatible with belief in a sovereign God and Christ as Lord, why diffusion of power and social equality rather than centralized power and social hierarchy are more compatible with Christian principles. Justifying democracy is made even more difficult by the fact that most modern democracies separate church and state, refuse to source lawmaking in Christian Scripture, and banish talk of God from founding documents and political debate.

In this book, we will consider three primary waves of negative Christian reaction to the theory and practice of democracy. The first came in the century or so after the French Revolution destroyed Catholic dominance in France and after Christianity began to weaken in nineteenth-century Germany. We will discuss what happened in those countries in chapters 5 and 6. The second wave came after the cultural-moral-social revolutions of the 1960s shattered traditional moral values in much of the Western world. The third wave, which may simply be an exacerbation of the 1960s phenomenon under the impact of social media and globalized politics, has occurred in the last ten years or so. We will look at developments in Russia, Poland, Hungary, Brazil, and the United States in chapters 7 through 11 as we consider these second and third waves of negative Christian reaction to recent cultural and political trends.

And Yet, Democracy Remains an Achievement Worth Defending

Many of the problems classically associated with democracy are not exclusive to democracy. They are basic problems of political order, exacerbated by what traditional Christian theology calls fallen (sinful) human nature. They must be addressed by any political system as it seeks to organize human affairs in community: the risk of tyranny (and of anarchy); the abuse of (or failure to exercise) power; acts of wrongdoing by government and governors; demagoguery that appeals to the basest human instincts; arbitrariness in decision-

making; the dangers of a leader making decisions based on irrationality, passion, stupidity, or prejudice; and the corrosive confusions,
divisions, and conflicts that so characterize human relationships.

As Reinhold Niebuhr noted, human beings have both God-
given capacities for self-government and such profound flaws
that we never fully solve society's problems, and every way of
organizing political communities has its own vulnerabilities. In
biblical tradition, we have a classic way of understanding this reality. Genesis 1 and 2 teach believers about our exalted God-given
status, responsibilities, and capacities, while Genesis 3 begins the
utterly realistic but ineffably sad account of human sinfulness in
relation to God and neighbor. This mix defines the human experience. Democracies will always reflect both human capacities and
human sinfulness.

I will engage seriously the criticisms of democracy that have
been offered by Christians over the centuries and that are inten-
sifying today. I will still assert, however, that in view of the track
record of the varied forms of government, democracy is not only
the best governance option heretofore developed, but in fact one of
the highest achievements of humanity. It is a great advance over
authoritarian power structures in which the fates of individuals
and entire societies have rested on the whims of a single ruler or a
small oligarchy. It took centuries to advance beyond authoritarian
government, and we dare not go backward now.

I believe that, without absolutizing democracy or any form
of human government, Christians can defend a modified understanding and practice of liberal democracy as congruent with key
Christian theological convictions and moral norms. We can likewise view democratic participation not as rebellion against Christ
or as a sidelining of our church commitments but as an expression
of both. I also firmly believe that Christian rejection of, or indifference to, democracy in past centuries and today has been one of our
greatest and most damaging mistakes. I will attempt to offer a fresh
Christian defense of democracy and consider some constructive re-

sources in our faith to support Christian participation in democratic self-government.

Today we are witnessing a sustained challenge to democracy, powerful enough to shake the foundations of many of our societies. This challenge combines elements old and new. We now deepen our investigation of it.

2

Alternatives and Threats to Democracy

Many forms of Government have been tried, and
will be tried in this world of sin and woe. No one pre-
tends that democracy is perfect or all-wise. Indeed
it has been said that democracy is the worst form of
Government except for all those other forms that
have been tried from time to time.

—Winston Churchill (1947)[1]

I am a democrat because I believe in the Fall of Man.

—C. S. Lewis (1943)[2]

Despite its roots in ancient Greece, democracy is a relative late-
comer to human politics, at least as a widely practiced form
of political organization.

The evidence is clear that once advances in agriculture made
possible the rise of sizable city-states in the ancient human past,
most societies centralized power in ruling elites, which eventually

1. Winston Churchill, British House of Commons, November 11, 1947,
cited in "Churchill's 'Democracy Is the Worst Form of Government . . . ,'"
richardlangworth.com.
2. Quoted in David T. Koyzis, *Political Visions and Illusions: A Survey
and Critique of Contemporary Ideologies* (Downers Grove, IL: InterVarsity
Press, 2003), 127.

evolved into absolutist monarchies, supported by local nobles and military leaders. This pattern is visible as early as ancient Sumer. The strongest of these city-states tended toward territorial aggression. Those that were successful became empires, their leaders styling themselves as all-powerful emperors. The first of these was Sargon of Akkad, in Mesopotamia (ca. 2300 BCE), and after that they just kept on coming, one bloody conquest after another.

Religion First Falls for Autocratic Power

Religion and politics were fused in most of these ancient kingdoms, with kings viewed as representatives of the gods or indeed as gods incarnate, and priests serving temples created by and for the political powers. Sacralization of existing dynasties, of course, reinforced the rulers' perceived legitimacy and thus their effective power. This entanglement of religion and statecraft, and the fantastic ideological, political, and economic powers associated with intertwined religious and political authorities, will be a major theme of this book. The attempt to separate religion from politics is a modern invention and one of the fundamental breaks between most forms of democracy and all prior forms of government.

It should be noted that one ancient society ended up looking rather different than the general pattern. The Hebrew Bible offers evidence of both religious sacralization of dynastic rule in Israel (in the Davidic dynasty) and the earlier, quite revolutionary idea that the rule of God over this particular people would occur through a covenant made by God with the people, and a Law that would apply to all. A key role of the prophets was to remind even the kings that they were not above that Law. This is just one way in which the Bible offers resources that devout believers found instructive as they stumbled toward democratic thinking—and that should still speak to us today.[3]

---

3. The best treatment I have read of the political implications of the

CHAPTER 2

The Birth of Modern Democracy

As we saw, modern democracy can be traced to beginnings in the seventeenth century, with stirrings visible even earlier. Many factors contributed to its rise. This included centuries of hard experience of the dangers of political absolutism, the diffusion of economic power through the rise of early capitalism, and growing emphasis on the needs and rights of the middle and lower classes in society, rather than simply the elites.

Anti-monarchical revolutions in what became the United States (1776) and France (1789) proved to be breakthroughs toward modern democracy. Over the ensuing centuries, democratization spread in Europe and in lands colonized by Europeans, though most of these democracies were deeply compromised by colonization itself—notably in the treatment of Indigenous groups, the enslavement of Africans, and the impact of centralized economic power (see ch. 13).

This early period is most realistically understood as *planting the seeds* of democracy, rather than as its full flowering. If we think of a democracy as an organic reality with a growth over time, we need not idealize its founding era—or founding documents—in any country.

The argument over whether democracy was the right or best political system remained lively long after the democratic revolutions of the late eighteenth century. The late nineteenth century saw the birth of Communism, a revolutionary movement that viewed existing forms of democracy as hopelessly compromised by capitalist economic power, a critique that has remained trenchant to this day. Communism became one of the premier antidemocratic political movements of the modern world, though with the twist of always purporting to represent "the people." Today, even in countries where

Hebrew Bible is Michael Walzer, *In God's Shadow: Politics in the Hebrew Bible* (New Haven: Yale University Press, 2012).

Communist ideology is essentially dead, its antidemocratic legacy is alive and well. Consider China and Russia as two premier examples. But also consider that the regimes that preceded Communism in these lands were hardly democratic.

The Twentieth-Century Crisis of Democracy

After World War I, antidemocratic right-wing movements strengthened, exploding in significance in the period lasting through World War II. Fascism emerged in Italy under Mussolini beginning in 1922, and Nazism, a form of fascism, took power in Germany in 1933 with Hitler. It must be noted that Hitler and the Nazis seized on a profound vulnerability of democracy—they used democratic elections to gain power, while fully intending to destroy democracy once in power.[4] Unless there is a mechanism within a democracy for politicians demonstrating clear antidemocratic tendencies to be disqualified from standing for office, this vulnerability will always exist within democracy.

Looked at as a whole, the period from 1920 to 1945 marked a profound challenge to democracy both from the left and from the right. Of course, the fascists were finally routed during World War II, and their vicious crimes against humanity thoroughly discredited them. It appeared such right-wing ideologies were doomed to the dustbin of history after 1945. But history routinely surprises us.

Democracy's Short-Lived Triumph

A look at any of the major founding documents of the United Nations after World War II reveals profound articulation of democratic and human rights norms both within nations and between them, as in the structures of the United Nations itself, a kind of democracy of

4. I am grateful for this reminder, offered by Bert Jan Lietaert Peerbolte, via private communication with the author.

nations. Rule of law, constitutionalism, human rights, separation of powers, and so on—they were all there, however imperfectly.

The birth of the European Union (EU) also solidified democratic norms as central to European identity. Today, nations that want to join the EU must meet strict democratic norms, and members who appear to be backsliding in their democratic practices are criticized and can be sanctioned. This has made the EU one of the major advocates for democracy in the world today. (Criticisms of the way the EU understands and attempts to advance democracy will be considered later.)

The collapse of the Soviet Union in 1991, leaving the then relatively poor China as the only major Communist country, seemed to reinforce the victory of democracy as the world's preferred political system. Its main opposition appeared to be radical Islamism, certainly not a broadly appealing political ideology.

Authoritarianism Makes a Comeback

Events since 2015, if not before, have now forced a reconsideration of this narrative of the victory of liberal democracy. While classic Communism does appear largely dead, authoritarian governments, ideologies, parties, and practices have surged, even in nations that appeared to have long consolidated democratic governments and cultures. This is the tendency that we are mainly considering in this book—the problem of democratic "backsliding" or "deconsolidation." The primary term we will use to contrast with democracy is "authoritarianism." Our concern is the deconsolidation of democracy into authoritarianism. Let us pause to consider the meaning of this key term.

Political authoritarianism is marked by the weakening or loss of popular sovereignty, the rejection or destruction of political pluralism, the entrenchment of a dominant individual or party at the center of political life, an end to genuinely free and fair elections, escalating attacks on political freedom and participation, and erosion of constitutionalism, the rule of law, civil liberties, and civil rights.[5] Authoritarianism begins with attacks on the norms and traditions of democracy by visible political leaders, and ends with the centralization of power and the dissolution of the division of powers.

Political authoritarianism can, in theory, come from the right or the left of the political spectrum. It is interesting that in polarized lands today, including the United States, both left and right accuse each other of authoritarian and antidemocratic tendencies. Check the best-seller list in the politics category any given day to see books in which both conservatives and liberals in the United States accuse each other of authoritarian designs. And history certainly offers plenty of evidence of authoritarian regimes both left and right.

Journalist and historian Anne Applebaum, who writes extensively about authoritarianism, argues that though authoritarian impulses can be seen on both sides, the *political* authoritarianism today "operating inside governments . . . [and] guiding important political parties" is mainly found on the right.[6] She documents her claims with references to Poland, in which she is a citizen (along with the United States), and several other nations. I find her research persuasive.

But this claim is hotly, bitterly, vehemently disputed on the conservative side. In many countries, conservatives argue that left-liberal authoritarianism is on the march not just from the commanding heights of culture, like the media and universities, but in liberal governments, the administrative apparatus of the modern state, and among liberal jurists in the judicial system.

For example, in an influential recent work, Polish philosopher Ryszard Legutko, who has served in cabinet posts in the Polish government as well as in the European Parliament, argues that the

5. Anne Applebaum, *Twilight of Democracy: The Seductive Lure of Authoritarianism* (New York: Anchor Books, 2021).
6. Applebaum, *Twilight of Democracy*, 18–19.

EU has moved from advancing liberal democracy in its original Lockean liberty-enhancing version to embracing an illiberal leftist ideology that now leverages vast EU powers to stamp out conservative religion and traditional moral values in democratic nations such as Poland.[7] As we will see in our country studies, similar claims are made by nearly every conservative authoritarian leader today, and they echo widely on the American right as well. We face a deeply polarized situation in which both sides claim that the other side is the one threatening democracy and being "illiberal" or even authoritarian.

It is hard to overstate how widely shared the belief in left-liberal "illiberal" authoritarianism is on the right, and not just the religious right, and certainly not just in the United States. Consider this comment from *Wall Street Journal* writer Barton Swaim, made in passing in a book review:

> Some liberals—typically the highly educated and privileged sort—tend to forget they are liberals and try to define righteousness for everybody. They do this by reallocating citizens' wealth according to their own ideals, regulating private economic behavior, dictating to local communities how they should govern themselves, imposing protean codes of correct speech and behavior on everyone else, and so on.[8]

And ponder this quote from Bret Stephens, one of the *New York Times*'s two resident conservative opinion writers:

> Then came the great American cultural revolution of the 2010s, in which traditional practices and beliefs—regarding same-sex

7. Ryszard Legutko, *The Demon in Democracy: Totalitarian Temptations in Free Societies*, trans. Teresa Adelson (New York: Encounter Books, 2018).

8. Barton Swaim, "'America's Philosopher' Review: The Key to John Locke," *Wall Street Journal*, August 5, 2022, https://tinyurl.com/292nthch.

marriage, sex-segregated bathrooms, personal pronouns, meritocratic ideals, race-blind rules, reverence for patriotic symbols, the rules of romance, the presumption of innocence and the distinction between equality of opportunity and outcome—became, more and more, not just passé but taboo. It's one thing for social mores to evolve over time, aided by respect for differences of opinion. It's another for them to be abruptly imposed by one side on another, with little democratic input but a great deal of moral bullying.[9]

Christian moral discomfort is sometimes motivated by the broad palette of mainstream conservative worries articulated by Swaim and Stephens. But as is to be expected, conservative Christians tend to have a specific focus on sex, gender, marriage, family, and children, that is, issues on which Christians believe they are adhering to authoritative and unchangeable religious convictions. The outrage level rises when Christians believe they are being belittled, intimidated, or governmentally coerced into sacrificing those convictions.

Meanwhile, among the conservative coalition are serious Christians, nominal Christians, and the frankly "irreligious right."[10] For the latter, their version of conservative outrage is often redolent of antisemitism, xenophobia, and patent racism, that is, flat-out ethno-nationalism. They are not hindered by whatever constraints on prejudice Christian teaching might once have offered. We will see this phenomenon in several of our country studies.

My analysis in this book will be that there is a global phenomenon today that can be called "authoritarian reactionary Christian politics." It is sourced by visceral and reactive discomfort against recent social changes as well as the perceived inability either to set

9. Bret Stephens, "I Was Wrong about Trump Voters," *New York Times*, July 24, 2022, 4.
10. Nate Hochman, "The Doctrine of the Irreligious Right," *New York Times*, June 5, 2022, 4–5.

the terms of their cultures or perhaps even to defend their way of life against cultural or governmental left-liberalism. Its strategies now frequently involve a pushing of democracy to or beyond its limits, a playing in (or beyond) the gray zone between legality and illegality, and a sliding *toward* autocracy and a sliding *away* from crucial democratic norms and practices.[11]

Still, I cannot accept a simple symmetry or parallelism between liberal and conservative authoritarianism. At least insofar as we are speaking about Freedom House–type democratic best practices criteria, the threat comes from the right.

Compare, for example, the postelection behavior of Democratic presidential candidate Al Gore after the razor-thin election of 2000 with that of Donald Trump after the not-especially-close election of 2020.[12] In 2000, the election came down to one state—Florida—in which the two candidates were within six hundred votes of each other. There were all kinds of problems with the count. The matter made its way to the Supreme Court, which then had a 5-4 conservative majority and ordered a stop to the vote counting in Florida by that same 5-4 majority. On constitutional grounds, the decision was dubious at best.

Under the circumstances, Al Gore had very good reasons to continue to contest the election. Instead, in his role as US vice president, Gore was the very person responsible for presiding over the official electoral vote tabulation that certified his own defeat in early January 2001. He did so, with good humor and without protest. He then showed up for George W. Bush's inauguration two weeks later. That is an example of honoring democratic norms, even when it is personally very hard. Can anyone reading this book imagine Donald Trump acting as Al Gore did in January 2001?

---

11. For this crucial problem-statement I credit Paul Peterson, via private communication with the author.

12. A compelling account is offered in Andrew Rice, *The Year That Broke America* (New York: HarperCollins, 2022).

Political authoritarianism is the antithesis of democracy. It weakens popular sovereignty, investing more and more power in the hands of one person or group. It undercuts the rule of law, as the dominant ones rise above accountability to the law and direct law enforcement to the maintenance of their power. It replaces temporary terms of office contested through scheduled free and fair elections with semi-permanent rule and sham elections or no elections. It blocks freedom of speech and free political participation, either through outright bans on critical speech or through intimidation. It misuses state power to eliminate political opposition, manipulating the criminal justice system and the judiciary to dominate or destroy adversaries. It renders civil rights and civil liberties protections null and void, perhaps in principle and certainly in practice.

How Democracies Die

Political scientists Steven Levitsky and Daniel Ziblatt, in their crucial 2018 book *How Democracies Die*, summarize authoritarian political behavior into four key categories:

- rejection of (or weak commitment to) democratic rules of the game
- denial of the legitimacy of political opponents
- toleration or encouragement of political violence
- readiness to curtail the civil liberties of opponents, including the media.[13]

Levitsky and Ziblatt argue that written constitutions and laws and a well-functioning judiciary are crucial in preventing antidemocratic authoritarianism, but that norms of mutual toleration and institu-

---

13. Steven Levitsky and Daniel Ziblatt, *How Democracies Die* (New York: Broadway Books, 2018), 23–24.

tional forbearance are "fundamental to a functioning democracy."[14] The classical tradition of "civic republicanism," which emphasizes the citizen virtues required to sustain politics aimed for the common good, calls this norm "civility."[15]

Again, we are reminded that democracy is a culture, not just a legal system. All cultures have norms. If these norms are functioning effectively, they do not often need to be discussed. It is only when norms are being violated or weakened that we remember that they are there, and why they are there. Various democratic norms are being eroded in many nations today. Some of us are remembering how important they are as we see them being trampled.

Democracy and authoritarianism exist on a spectrum and are best understood in dynamic terms. Democratic practices in any polity can range from robust to nonexistent, and at any time democracy can be described as strengthening or weakening. Freedom House ranks nations on a 0 to 100 democracy scale, and always presents the *direction of movement* when describing what is going on in a country. That direction is crucial. Caring citizens must always be monitoring it.

The politics of a country is a living thing, and at any moment can be moving in more healthy or less healthy directions. The concern for many of us is that the political direction of many nations, including some with a substantial democratic tradition, has been trending away from democracy. The United States offers a breathtaking example.

Tyranny, Fascism, Populism, and Nationalism

Before moving ahead, let us define a few other terms that are sometimes used in the discussion of authoritarian political trends and will make occasional appearances here as appropriate.

14. Levitsky and Ziblatt, *How Democracies Die*, 101–2.
15. John Maynor, "Civic Republicanism," Britannica, https://tinyurl.com/mpscr7sj.

Yale historian Timothy Snyder uses the ancient word "tyranny" as the central term in his widely noted 2017 book, *On Tyranny*. He defines it as "the usurpation of power by a single individual or group, or the circumvention of law by rulers for their own benefit."[16] Tyranny as thus defined creates the conditions for authoritarian rule.

Long after it seemed dead and buried, the term "fascism" has been making a comeback—not as the self-description of authoritarian politicians, but as an epithet applied by their enemies, or as an analytical category applied by scholars as fitting some of the data in front of us.

Three books released during the political convulsions of the last few years have made fascism their central category. The late US secretary of state Madeleine Albright, in her compelling *Fascism: A Warning* (2018), sketches fascism's characteristics as follows: "an extreme form of authoritarian rule . . . linked to rabid nationalism . . . power begins with the leader, and the people have no rights . . . a Fascist is someone who . . . claims to speak for a whole nation or group, is unconcerned with the rights of others, and is willing to use whatever means are necessary—including violence—to achieve his or her goals."[17]

Jason Stanley, in his 2018 work *How Fascism Works*, describes fascism as "ultranationalism of some variety (ethnic, religious, cultural), with the nation represented in the person of an authoritarian leader who speaks on its behalf."[18] Stanley helpfully distinguishes between "fascist politics" and a "fascist state." Fascist politics is a mechanism to gain power; it may or may not succeed in metastasizing into the creation of a fascist state, as in Nazi Germany.

16. Timothy Snyder, *On Tyranny: Twenty Lessons from the Twentieth Century* (London: Bodley Head, 2017), 10.

17. Madeleine Albright, *Fascism: A Warning* (New York: HarperPerennial, 2018), 11–12.

18. Jason Stanley, *How Fascism Works: The Politics of Us and Them* (New York: Random House, 2020), xxviii.

This distinction makes it possible to name fascist political strategies or tendencies even when those wielding them have not succeeded (yet) in remaking their nation's political system.

Stanley summarizes the characteristics of fascist politics as follows: real history is displaced by a mythic past, truth and reality are displaced by propaganda, anti-intellectualism displaces expertise, conspiracy theories and lies displace truth and history, a hierarchical vision displaces any vision of human equality, a sense of victimhood is encouraged on the part of majority populations as a response to any gains for minority groups, "law and order" politics emphasize tough policing of lawless others, sexual anxiety is stirred up related to perceived threats to patriarchy and masculinity, and members of dehumanized groups are described as lazy dependents. Fascism is, in short, characterized by myths, propaganda, hierarchy, anger, patriarchy, violence, sexual anxiety, and dehumanization.

In his subtle and profound work *A Brief History of Fascist Lies* (2020), historian Federico Finchelstein situates lying at the very center of fascism: "Lying is a feature of fascism in a way that is not true of . . . other political traditions. . . . Fascists consider their lies to be at the service of simple absolute truths, which are in fact bigger lies."[19] Threading this analysis of systemic mendacity through his discussion of fascism, Finchelstein ends up with a treatment of fascism that looks in some ways similar to what Stanley offers, but goes deeper into its irrationality.

For Finchelstein, fascism makes knowledge a matter of faith, beginning with faith in the myth of the leader. Fascism is rooted in anti-Enlightenment irrationalism, a modern counterrevolutionary movement against liberalism, democracy, and Marxism, which we will often encounter in these pages. In fascism, the leader is the embodiment of the nation and of truth. Enemies of the leader

---

19. Federico Finchelstein, *A Brief History of Fascist Lies* (Oakland: University of California Press, 2020), 3.

are defined as enemies of truth, and of the nation, who must be destroyed by violence. The leader is always right and owns the truth, a truth beyond reality, inquiry, and history. Truth is attained through revelation from the leader, who incarnates the soul of the people. Dictatorship is redefined as "true" democracy because the leader embodies the people. Political violence and the desire for a kind of redemptive destruction come to characterize fascism, as fascist policies attempt to create new realities to correspond with their mythologies. For example, anti-Jewish fascists have dreamt of a world without Jews and then at times have enacted horrific policies to turn this dream into reality.

Finchelstein also offers a foray into the relationship between fascism and modern "populism," another term much in circulation during these dark days. He treats modern populism as "an authoritarian understanding of democracy that reworked the legacy of fascism after 1945. . . . After the defeat of fascism, populism emerged as a form of post-fascism, which reformulated fascism for democratic times . . . populism is fascism adapted to democracy."[20]

Definitions of populism take various forms, though most often they tend to view populism negatively, as a threat to democracy.[21] Cas Mudde and Cristóbal Kaltwasser define populism as "a thin-centered ideology that considers society to be ultimately separated into two homogeneous and antagonistic camps, the 'pure people' versus 'the corrupt elite,' and which argues that politics should

20. Finchelstein, *Brief History of Fascist Lies*, 6.

21. It should be noted that though negative assessments of populism tend to predominate, there are other approaches. Luke Bretherton, for example, understands populism as "an inherent, and often benign, feature of democratic politics," sometimes offering a kind of course correction when democracy faces a "crisis of representation." He goes on to add, however, that "as with all forms of politics, it can become toxic," and "populism as a *regime of statecraft* is rarely, if ever, democratic." Bretherton, *Christ and the Common Life: Political Theology and the Case for Democracy* (Grand Rapids: Eerdmans, 2019), 403, 432, 437.

be an expression of the . . . general will of the people."[22] Michael Kazin describes American populism in particular as "a language whose speakers conceive of ordinary people as a noble assemblage not bounded narrowly by class; view their elite opponents as self-serving and undemocratic; and seek to mobilize the former against the latter."[23] Marcia Pally defines populism as "a way of understanding and developing solutions to economic, way-of-life, and status-loss duress which relies on an 'us-them' binary." Ideas about government, society, and elites that exist in a nation's culture and history help shape populist constructions of "us" and "them," and help direct "populist anger" toward specific targets.[24]

My summary of these accounts would be that—at least when it turns toxic—populism as an ideology interprets frustrating dimensions of reality by creating or exacerbating us-them antagonisms in society, while populism as a strategy manipulates the frustrations of a group of citizens who perceive themselves to be under duress, and then directs those frustrations at designated targets, all while accruing political power to the effective populist agitator. Democracies are clearly quite vulnerable to destructive populist manipulation.

Finchelstein argues that extreme populism demonstrates fascist impulses and can threaten democracy itself. Describing "Trumpism," but with other examples in mind, Finchelstein sees "an extreme form of postfascism, an antiliberal, and often anticonstitutional, authoritarian democracy."[25] His historical account sees populism as

22. Cas Mudde and Cristóbal Rovira Kaltwasser, *Populism: A Very Short Introduction* (New York: Oxford University Press, 2017), 6. "Thin-centered" means "to have a restricted morphology, which necessarily appears attached to—and sometimes is even assimilated into—other ideologies."

23. Michael Kazin, *The Populist Persuasion: An American History* (New York: Basic Books, 1995), 1. See also John B. Judis, *The Populist Explosion: How the Great Recession Transformed American and European Politics* (New York: Columbia Global Reports, 2016).

24. Marcia Pally, *White Evangelicals and Right-Wing Populism: How Did We Get Here?* (London: Routledge, 2022), 21.

25. Finchelstein, *Brief History of Fascist Lies*, 108.

succeeding fascism after 1945 but apparently always at risk of giving way once again to fascism if the conditions are right.

Finally, let's focus on the terms "patriotism," "nationalism," and "ultranationalism." If we define patriotism in basic terms as a feeling of attachment, loyalty, pride, and devotion to one's country, then nationalism is patriotism taken up a notch or two. It is an intensification of patriotism, adding negative judgments on the value or worth of other nations/peoples, lack of concern about the well-being of those in other lands, and perhaps an expansionist vision of one's own nation's proper role in the world vis-à-vis other countries. Ultranationalism might be described as extreme, manic, dangerous nationalism, accentuating both the puffed-up sense of the value of one's own nation and the xenophobic, even dehumanizing view of others. When patriotism becomes nationalism, and especially when nationalism becomes ultranationalism, trouble is surely on its way, as love of country becomes a monstrous, soul-eating force prepared to violate moral boundaries and target perceived national enemies with violence.

If the "nation," as Stanley suggests parenthetically above, is identified with a particular ethnic, religious, or cultural group within it, then nationalism and ultranationalism also pose a threat to the interests and rights of groups *within* a country—and not just outside it—that are perceived as not fully belonging to the nation. Anti-Jewish ultranationalists in Nazi Germany, for example, defined German "Jews" in a particular way, locating this group as non-citizens, then as non-humans, then as worthy of death. Jews have often been targeted by this kind of dangerous, exclusivist nationalism, as have Blacks, immigrants, and other perceived outsiders in many lands. Thus, nationalism and ultranationalism are threats not just to those outside the host nation but to those within as well.

The special concern of this book is the role of Christians and Christianity in relation to all these negative trends. The claim here is that the slide away from democracy and toward right-wing authoritarianism in nations including Russia, Poland, Hungary, Brazil, and the United States today, and other nations in the past, is connected to and exacerbated by the historic and contemporary attitudes of a substantial part of the Christian populations of these lands. There are "Christian" versions of populism, fascism, authoritarianism, and nationalism. There is also a "Christian" history and politics that is acutely relevant to the antidemocratic tendencies that concern so many of us today. This is where we now turn.

3

Authoritarian Reactionary Christianity

> Is it not true that . . . each and every one of [modern
> society's] three progressive thrusts has been followed
> by ideological counterthrusts of extraordinary force?
> And have not these counterthrusts been at the origin
> of convulsive social and political struggles often lead-
> ing to setbacks for the intended progressive programs
> as well as to much human suffering and misery?
>
> —Albert O. Hirschman (1991)[1]

> It is the first step in sociological wisdom to recognize,
> that the major advances in civilization are processes
> which all but wreck the societies in which they occur.
>
> —Alfred North Whitehead (1927)[2]

"Authoritarian reactionary Christianity" (ARC) will be the
main term I will use to attempt to name the version of Christian politics that leads to support for or indifference to democratic

---

1. Albert O. Hirschman, *The Rhetoric of Reaction* (Cambridge, MA:
Belknap Press of Harvard University Press, 1991), 2–3.
2. Alfred North Whitehead, *Symbolism: Its Meaning and Effect* (1927;
repr., New York: Fordham University Press, 1985), 88.

backsliding. This is my coinage; I have not seen the problem named this way by another author. At this moment, at least in the US setting, the term "Christian nationalism" has become the primary shorthand to name and critique problematic Christian politics. In this chapter, I want to propose that "authoritarian reactionary Christianity" may offer a broader historical and cultural framework to name and understand what we are seeing in much of the world today. Labels matter if they enhance understanding, reduce disorientation, and empower response. That is my goal here.

Authoritarian Reactionary Christianity

First, we turn to authoritarianism. Recall that in the last chapter we described political authoritarianism as weakening popular sovereignty and centralizing power in one person or group, undercutting the rule of law and free and fair elections, blocking or limiting freedom of speech, misusing state power to weaken or eliminate political opposition, manipulating the criminal justice system and the judiciary, and weakening essential civil rights and civil liberties protections.

It can be documented easily that in multiple countries conservative Christians have demonstrated susceptibility toward or active support for political authoritarianism as just described. We will consider such tendencies in the current or very recent politics of Russia, Poland, Hungary, Brazil, and the United States. Taking a longer historical view, we will also consider older examples in late nineteenth- to early twentieth-century France and Germany. While there have been examples of self-identified Christians supporting left-wing authoritarian movements and governments—for example, in the polarized politics of some Latin American countries—the far more common paradigm has been right-wing Christian authoritarianism. In any case, this is a book about the latter.

It can also be documented easily that many Christians tend toward religious and moral authoritarianism quite apart from any political authoritarianism. It is striking that in his recent book attacking liberal democracy as practiced in the European Union today, Polish philosopher-politician Ryszard Legutko lists as one of his critiques that it purposely undercuts "traditional moral and cultural authoritarianism."[3] Here authoritarianism is used as a positive term to describe traditional Polish Catholic ways of living. This may strike the modern liberal ear as odd, but "authoritarianism" as a positive value term associated with Christian living is used in other conservative Christian traditions as well.

Adapting our definition of political authoritarianism, we will describe religious authoritarianism as an understanding and practice of truth and authority in religious institutions in which hierarchical and centralized power prevails throughout the religious system. A monarchical or perhaps oligarchical power structure is treated as vested by God with authoritative access to ultimate Truth. This sacralized Authority is understood to have the power to proclaim sacred truth, interpret sacred texts, and command communal obedience. In the most authoritarian environments, no venue exists for individual or communal participation in the truth-discernment, interpretation, and proclamation process, as well as no real avenue for protest or appeal. Sometimes an environment of intimidation exists that further stifles dissent.

In many religious traditions, and not just in Christian ones, the role of the people is to receive and obey authoritative teaching, not to debate what to believe. Many believers take great comfort in this submission, and in not having to wonder what is true and right—especially in a world full of religious and moral conflict and confusion. Meanwhile, multiple biblical teachings urge such submission to authoritative church teachings and those who offer them. Consider texts such as this: "Obey your leaders and submit to them, for they are keeping watch over your souls as those who will give an account" (Heb. 13:17).

3. Ryszard Legutko, *The Demon in Democracy: Totalitarian Temptations in Free Societies,* trans. Teresa Adelson (New York: Encounter Books, 2018), 93.

Speaking only of Christians, and to Christians, we must face the fact that organized Christianity, born two millennia ago, continues to carry forward authoritarian governance structures in many of its institutional expressions. The level of authoritarianism exists along a spectrum, and the voice of the people can wax or wane in its influence.

Roman Catholicism, for example, demonstrated a move away from both internal and political authoritarianism during the Second Vatican Council (1962–1965), a process with complex roots that continues to occupy contemporary scholarship.[4] The extent of the Catholic Church's internal democratizing process continues to be debated; currently a "synodal" process is being undertaken under the leadership of Pope Francis, which involves a significant effort to listen to the people of the Church. This is undoubtedly a democratizing initiative, and it not surprisingly has been met with suspicion by authoritarian voices in the Catholic Church.[5] The question of the relationship between the church authorities (the magisterium) and the people never goes away in Catholicism, though it is hard to gainsay the conclusion that it remains primarily a top-down, nondemocratic religious institution.

Many forms of Protestantism also centralize power in bishops, elders, and pastors. In Protestantism, the claim to biblical rather than merely "human" authority has the potential to limit authoritarianism,

4. Sarah Shortall, for example, finds roots in the *nouvelle théologie* movement in France in the early to mid-twentieth century. See Shortall, *Soldiers of God in a Secular World: Catholic Theology in Twentieth-Century French Politics* (Cambridge, MA: Harvard University Press, 2021). John McGreevy identifies French theologian (later exiled in the United States) Jacques Maritain as especially significant in the Vatican's belated embrace of democracy. McGreevy, "'Natural Enemies' No More," *Commonweal*, July/August 2022, 24–28.

5. McGreevy, "Natural Enemies," 28. For further discussion, see John W. O'Malley, "Papal Upgrades," *America*, July/August 2022, 39–41, and Robert W. McElroy, "Keep Talking," *America*, July/August 2022, 28. McElroy has recently been appointed a cardinal by Pope Francis.

as the Bible is in the hands of the whole people. But this only works in those Protestant churches and sects that seriously invest interpretive power in *the entire believing community*, rather than in elders or the pastor. This is the historic Baptist paradigm, to which we will return in chapter 12. But it has never become the majority Protestant pattern.

The claim here is that Christianity, with its ancient roots, carried forward many authoritarian, pre-democratic, and even antidemocratic tendencies into the modern world—centuries after politics in many historically Christian lands embraced democratic norms. I am not arguing that every structure in human life must be governed democratically; this will not and cannot ever be the case. However, I am suggesting that it is significant that majorities of Christians participate in nondemocratic and sometimes profoundly authoritarian religious institutions. It may be that where a significant number of Christian groups and individuals have not democratized their understanding of the organization of power in human communities, these Christians can unwittingly function as antidemocratic incubators in modern societies.

Sometimes antidemocratic political thought is explicitly taught in traditionalist Christian communities. I know it because I have seen it, in the curriculum taught to my children in a Christian school they attended for a while. That was twenty years ago, so I checked online to see if the curriculum is still in use. It is. Under the title "The Principle Approach," this widely used curriculum for Christian school and homeschool teaching claims that "the form of government proven to best protect life and property is a Christian constitutional federal republic."[6] And: "Civil government takes into account man's sinful nature and exists to secure the God-given rights of the individual. Civil government is based upon God's law, not the will of the people."[7]

---

6. Leslie Schmucker, "What Is a Principle Approach School?" Dayspring Christian Academy, https://tinyurl.com/pw56h3f4.

7. "The Principle Approach," Dayspring Christian Academy, https://tinyurl.com/2tvyedzx.

As of this writing, some emerging Republican leaders and candidates in the United States are expressing this rhetoric nearly exactly. Their vision is often of an end to the separation of church and state and an officially Christian government attempting to enforce biblical laws.[8]

An earlier and cruder version of this teaching is called Christian Reconstructionism.[9] Following the leadership of men like the late Gary North, Reconstructionists teach that US society should be governed by (their understanding of) Old Testament law, including, for example, the death penalty for gay sex.[10] I once was a guest on a US Christian radio station in which my segment directly followed an interview with a man who advocated such a law. I was shocked. While Gary North died in 2022, his ideas have not disappeared. They are in the news again as they are being articulated as live options on the right wing of US Christian politics.

It is interesting that the main group in the United States expressing fears that the US Muslim community constitutes a threatening antidemocratic population are the far more numerous fundamentalist and evangelical Christians who could pose a much more profound threat to democracy. It is not fundamentalist Muslims who today are serious candidates for federal and statewide offices in the United States. It is Christians who are positioning themselves to remake our 240-year-old democratic and church/state arrangements.

Authoritarian *Reactionary* Christianity

Now let us consider the term "reactionary." In his classic work *The Rhetoric of Reaction*, Princeton professor Albert Hirschman traces

8. See Elizabeth Dias, "The Far-Right Christian Quest for Power: 'We Are Seeing Them Emboldened,'" *New York Times*, July 8, 2022, https://tinyurl.com/2p82uj5j.

9. See Julie J. Ingersoll, *Building God's Kingdom: Inside the World of Christian Reconstruction* (Oxford: Oxford University Press, 2015).

10. Sam Roberts, "Gary North, Apostle of Bible-Based Economics, Dies," *New York Times*, March 4, 2022, https://tinyurl.com/4knmx22p.

the use of the terms "reaction" and "reactionary" in modern political thought to Benjamin Constant's tract *Des réactions politiques* (1797), which denounced the Thermidorian Reaction in the period from July 27, 1794, to November 2, 1795, following the Reign of Terror during the French Revolution.[11] (See chapter 5.) Constant's position was that the French Revolution, despite its bloody excesses, marked decisive forward progress in human history—a major Enlightenment theme, by the way—and thus those who wished to turn back the clock were negatively assessed as "reactionaries."

Hirschman says that he wishes to avoid using reaction and reactionary as a negative value judgment, but simply to describe a phenomenon consistently visible in politics—dramatic changes have tended to evoke equally dramatic reactions against them, each "thrust" evoking a "counterthrust." Even if most would consider a change to represent progress, there will always be those who react negatively and view the change as disastrous. Think of the end of slavery, or women's suffrage, or public education for girls as well as boys. Each evoked counterthrusts, negative reactions.

To the extent that reactionaries are attempting to block changes embraced by the overwhelming majority as tremendous steps forward for human progress, they will be viewed quite negatively by most of those around them. The reactionaries, in turn, will sometimes develop an embattled and defiant streak as they continue to fight against, in Hirschman's words, "an intellectual climate in which a positive value attaches to whatever lofty objective is placed on the social agenda by self-proclaimed 'progressives.'"[12] There could hardly be a better sketch of conservative resentment as we find it in many nations today.

The argument I am making in this book is that religious, moral, and, most relevant here, political authoritarianism among Christians is often activated by a strongly negative reaction to modernity, democracy, and pluralism, or to certain cultural, moral, political,

11. Hirschman, *Rhetoric of Reaction*, 8-9.
12. Hirschman, *Rhetoric of Reaction*, 11.

or legal developments in democratic societies, which progressive forces treat as great advances for progress but traditionalist Christians reject. This negative reaction can then fuel latent or open political authoritarianism.

When a negative reaction to modern cultural and political developments hardens into a permanent posture of Christian disdain for modernity and democracy, I believe that it can be fairly named reactionary, a term I use here both descriptively and as a negative value judgment. I judge it negatively because, from the perspective of Christian ethics, I believe that a blanket posture of negative reaction is a too simple form of engagement with culture, and a too pessimistic response to social change—even the dramatic social changes we have seen in our cultures since the 1960s. I judge it negatively because it also yields bad fruit; it tempts toward authoritarianism and other toxicities that are its fellow travelers, such as conspiracy theories, gutter politics, and even militia violence.

As we will see multiple times in this book, this reactionary Christian tendency has been visible since the very origins of the modern world. The rise of reason and science and weakening of religious authority, the rise of democracy and weakening of monarchy, the rise of worldview pluralism and weakening of the hegemony of Christian ways of organizing reality, the enfranchisement of non-majority religious believers and non-Christians and end of majoritarian Christian power, the rise of secular institutions and weakening of the (dominant) church—all have routinely evoked strong Christian opposition. Powerful Christian institutions and many mainstream Christians reacted negatively to all such developments when they emerged beginning as early as the seventeenth and eighteenth centuries. What often (not always, but often) resulted was reactionary antidemocratic tendencies and susceptibility to authoritarian politics as part of an overall allergic reaction to the modern world. This was first-wave antidemocratic reaction.

But new waves of Christian reaction have been unleashed as social changes considered threatening by some Christians have accelerated. Even some Christians who over decades or centuries had perhaps more or less come to terms with what might loosely be named as liberal, pluralistic, secular, democratic modernity now are showing susceptibility to religiously and morally motivated authoritarian reaction.

Especially when these Christians believe themselves to be losing significant cultural influence, facing moral or political threats to their families or institutions, and being offered the opportunity to (re)gain cultural and political power, they can prove susceptible to authoritarian, antidemocratic, Christian theocratic politics. They might even come to believe that they have the rare, God-given opportunity within the secular modern world to bend the "arc of history" backward. That might be a way of remembering the term *authoritarian reactionary Christianity*: a form of politics attempting to bend the **arc** of history backward toward a premodern world of Christian political and cultural hegemony.

Authoritarianism in Christianity is a feature, not a bug, and it is unlikely to change in most Christian quarters anytime soon. Perhaps on its own it is a problem mainly to those inside the community who wish for more voice, more breathing room, more freedom. But when Christian authoritarianism hooks up with fierce cultural reaction, when it is highly politicized, and when that politicization becomes genuinely antidemocratic, it can become a profound problem for the society as a whole.[13]

Below is a chart that summarizes my description of each dimension of my paradigm: authoritarian, reactionary Christianity and its political expressions. Readers might want to mark this page for consultation in later chapters.

13. I am grateful to Ron Sanders for this formulation, via private communication with the author.

CHAPTER 3

Authoritarian Reactionary Christian Politics

Authoritarian (political)	Reactionary
• rejection/weakening of democratic rules	• counterthrust to dramatic social changes
• denial of legitimacy of opponents	• opposed to end of throne/altar regimes
• toleration/encouragement of political violence	• opposed to "liberalism" & "secularism"
• readiness to curtail civil liberties & rights	• embattled & defiant minority spirit
• usurpation & misuse of state power by rulers lamenting lost cultural uniformity	• posture of nostalgia & perhaps despair
• circumvention & manipulation of law	• discomfort with pluralism & diversity
• weakening of popular sovereignty	• rejection of democratic egalitarianism
• centralization, lack of checks on power	• effort to bend the arc of history backward
• often: paternalist/masculinist vision	• may be explicitly "counterrevolutionary"
	• culture wars effort to take back the nation
Authoritarian (religious-moral)	• liberals as enemies in battle of good versus evil
• centralized power vis-à-vis religious truth	
• top-down structures prevail	
• little avenue for protest or dissent	
• emphasis on submission to authority	
• environment of intimidation may exist	

Christian	Authoritarian Reactionary Christian Politics
• official church authorities	• antidemocratic politics taught to believers
• self-identified Christian populations	• anti–church/state separation
• politicians deploy Christian rhetoric	• "culture wars" must be ended via victory
• seek Christian norm-setter role in culture	• impose "biblical" or "natural" law
• seek Christian institutional power/favor	• override majorities/rights in God's name
• weakened acceptance of religious diversity	• may express as Christian nation-ism
• may turn toward open antisemitism	• may fuse with racism and xenophobia
• may turn toward anti-Muslim stance	• may fuse with nationalism/militarism
• moral traditionalism on gender, sex, family	• often anti-LGBTQ+, anti–gender equality
• may draw upon biblical apocalypticism	• may adopt conspiracy thinking
• nation as "Christian," "chosen," or "holy land"	• may adopt holy war militancy & violence
• may be expressed heretically/immorally	• may be aided by irreligious rightist groups

Considering Christian Nationalism and
Christian Populism

I believe "authoritarian reactionary Christianity" is the best umbrella term for what we are witnessing today and have witnessed before in Christian politics. In this section, I want to consider several other terms scholars recently have developed that, one might say, live in the same neighborhood, as all are attempting to name and describe problematic forms of Christian politics. In general, these terms take up concepts that we considered in the last chapter, like nationalism and populism, and add "religious" or "Christian" as an adjective.

Let's begin with the term "religious nationalism," as found in the work of Mark Juergensmeyer and others.[14] Centering on Juergensmeyer, we find that he was a pioneer of turn-of-the-twenty-first-century scholarship on religious militancy and violence. This included religious terrorism, which he defined as "public acts of violence . . . for which religion has provided the motivation, the justification, the organization, and the world view."[15] He further specified "religious nationalism" as having to do with occasions in which "religion becomes fused with violent expressions of social aspirations, personal pride, and movements for political change."[16] Thus, religious nationalism, for Juergensmeyer, is one expression of or context for religious violence, one in which religious and nationalist aspirations become fused and together motivate the use of a violence understood as sacred.

---

14. Mark Juergensmeyer, *Terror in the Mind of God: The Global Rise of Religious Violence* (Berkeley: University of California Press, 2000). Related literature from that period includes R. Scott Appleby, *The Ambivalence of the Sacred: Religion, Violence, and Reconciliation* (Lanham, MD: Rowman & Littlefield, 2000); Charles Kimball, *When Religion Becomes Evil: Five Warning Signs* (New York: HarperCollins, 2003). Juergensmeyer's recent summative reflections on these issues can be found as *God at War: A Meditation on Religion and Warfare* (New York: Oxford University Press, 2020).

15. Juergensmeyer, *Terror in the Mind of God*, 7.

16. Juergensmeyer, *Terror in the Mind of God*, 10.

In the past several years, the leading category being used in scholarship and in public discussion to describe disturbing political trends among US Christians has been Christian nationalism, which was spearheaded by an influential 2020 book by sociologists Samuel Perry and Andrew Whitehead, *Taking America Back for God*.[17] Today, the term is used constantly in public conversation and debate. It is as ubiquitous as the term "Christian Right" was a generation or two ago.

One fundamental complication with this term "Christian nationalism" is that Whitehead and Perry were talking about something different than religious nationalism as defined by Juergensmeyer. They helpfully shorthand their meaning early in their book when they call it "Christian nation-ism." With this term, they want to name "a commitment to a vision of American civic life and polity as closely intertwined with an identitarian, politically conservative strain of Christianity."[18] Whitehead and Perry put it this way:

> The "Christianity" of Christian nationalism represents something more than religion . . . it includes assumptions of nativism, white supremacy, patriarchy, and heteronormativity, along with divine sanction for authoritarian control and militarism. It is as ethnic and political as it is religious. Understood in this light, Christian nationalism contends that America has been and always should be distinctively "Christian" (reflecting this fuller, more nuanced sense of the term) from top to bottom—in its self-identity, interpretations of its own history, sa-

17. Andrew L. Whitehead and Samuel L. Perry, *Taking America Back for God: Christian Nationalism in the United States* (New York: Oxford University Press, 2020). The book has spawned a massive literature. Two recent contributions are Philip S. Gorski and Samuel L. Perry, *The Flag and the Cross: White Christian Nationalism and the Threat to American Democracy* (New York: Oxford University Press, 2022), and Paul D. Miller, *The Religion of American Greatness: What's Wrong with Christian Nationalism* (Downers Grove, IL: InterVarsity Press, 2022).

18. Whitehead and Perry, *Taking America Back for God*, x–xi.

cred symbols, cherished values, and public policies—and aims to keep it that way.[19]

Thus, Christian-nation ideology is the belief that America is and ought to be a white, straight, native-born, hetero-male-led, militarist, authoritarian nation, and that this is what it "means" to be a "Christian nation." However odious this vision, if this is Christian nationalism, it need not be inclined to or intertwined with the religio-political extremism or violence that Juergensmeyer writes about.

Recent events, however, especially the role of extremist Christians in supporting the January 6 insurrection, have revealed an element open to deploying violence in the name of its Christian political/religious vision. It may be that a group within the Christian-nation subculture described by Whitehead and Perry a few years ago has in the meantime proved to be mobilizable for religious-nationalist violence.

Or—and here is a more pessimistic take—it may be that these violent religious-nationalist potentialities have recently been *revived* after lying dormant for a generation. If one thinks about the long history of white ethno-nationalist violence in the United States, from slavery all the way through the civil rights movement, and then one looks at the seamiest part of the Christian-nation movement, we are in the same ballpark. I am tentatively suggesting that, by now, Christian-nation ideology and extremist white religious nationalism may be converging in the United States.

Marcia Pally, in her book *White Evangelicals and Right-Wing Populism*, works with the category of populism to describe the reality. She describes evangelical right-wing populism as rooted in economic, way-of-life, and status-loss duress.[20] Pally suggests that

19. Whitehead and Perry, *Taking America Back for God*, 10. It is fascinating that, during the writing of this book, not only has the use of the term "Christian nationalism" continued to become the journalistic default in the United States, but it has also begun to be explicitly embraced by some right-wing politicians and Christian leaders.

20. Marcia Pally, "White Evangelicals and American Right-Wing Popu-

one primary reason fundamentalists and evangelicals supported Donald Trump was their deep responsiveness to his economic, moral, and religious populism. "Make America Great Again" meant, for him and for these followers, to restore (white) Christians to the economic and cultural center of US life by reducing "big government" and limiting government regulation, by pushing back against societal trends perceived as sinful or that unseated white Christians as the nation's norm-setters (like LGBTQ+ acceptance), and, not incidentally, by claiming to protect the jobs of the economically precarious from outsourcing abroad or being taken by undocumented immigrants.

Populist politicians, and not just in the United States, have had great success stirring up some Christians by claiming that elites are "taking their country away" and that it is time to take it back. Sometimes populists emphasize the dangers of immigration, sometimes economic losses, and almost always they inflame anxiety among formerly dominant Christian groups that their ways of life and social status are losing ground or even being attacked. This is what we might call right-wing Christian culture-wars populism. The LGBTQ+ inclusion issue has been deployed repeatedly by populists in many lands for this purpose. It appears, at this time, to be the ultimate populist trope.

Christian nationalism (Christian-nation ideology) and Christian right-wing populism are best understood as religio-political mentalities currently generating active strategies for gaining power in the United States, and undoubtedly in other countries as well. But authoritarian reactionary Christianity may offer a broader framework for naming the historical-cultural reality of this moment. Nearly one-fourth of the way through the twenty-first century, tens of millions of Christian people are attempting to bend the

---

lism: The Evolutions of an Ethics," *Journal of the Society of Christian Ethics*, forthcoming 2023. Her book-length treatment, cited earlier, is Pally, *White Evangelicals and Right-Wing Populism: How Did We Get Here?* (London: Routledge, 2022).

arc of history backward, attempting a religious counterrevolution to the secular revolutions that they cannot accept and by which they feel threatened.

Our next step will take us to political philosopher Michael Walzer. He helped me solidify a paradigm of secular revolution and religious counterrevolution as a paradigm for understanding authoritarian reactionary Christianity.j

4

Secular Revolutions and Religious Counterrevolutions

For the settler militants, the nation-state as it exists today is simply an instrument for promoting God's politics. . . . They look forward to a time . . . when democracy (an alien Western form of government) will be replaced by an authentically Jewish religious regime that will lead Jews back to a life based on the Torah.

—Michael Walzer (2015)[1]

In 2015, Princeton political philosopher Michael Walzer published *The Paradox of Liberation: Secular Revolutions and Religious Counterrevolutions*. The title itself immediately arrested me, as it crystallized an intuition that runs somewhat parallel to what Walzer is doing in this 2015 book. I believe that the United States and several other countries are currently experiencing religious counterrevolutions to the cultural and moral (often labeled "secular")[2] revolutions

1. Michael Walzer, *The Paradox of Liberation: Secular Revolutions and Religious Counterrevolutions* (New Haven: Yale University Press, 2015), 60.
2. I acknowledge that there is considerable scholarly debate over the terms "secular" and "secularization" and whether the thesis of Western secularization is actually accurate. But for our purposes, we can keep it fairly simple. "Secular," for Walzer's analysis in this book, means a political effort that is explicitly and intentionally opposed to religious involvement

that exploded in the 1960s—revolutions related to gender, sexuality, marriage, race, immigration, media, technology, patriotism, war, abortion, contraception, and so on. These religious counterrevolutions are of massive importance, profoundly affecting culture, law, and politics. Unfortunately, they also sometimes display antidemocratic tendencies, as religious counterrevolutionaries sometimes consider their cause so important that they do not always respect democratic boundaries. My claim is that contemporary threats to democracy are intimately related to the dynamic of secular revolution and religious counterrevolution.

Cycles of Negative Reaction

But this is also true in a different way in relation to the first wave of antidemocratic Christian reaction beginning more than two hundred years ago. The concept of secular revolution triggering religious counterrevolution is just as relevant in earlier periods, but it needs further refinement. Its applicability is especially clear when one considers the harshly anti-Christian revolutions of the late eighteenth century in France and of the early twentieth-century Communist regimes. In France and in Russia, for example, revolutions explicitly targeted the old Christendom regimes that had mixed church, state, and aristocracy in an arrangement going back to medieval times. The revolutionaries targeted the Catholic Church in France and the Orthodox Church in Russia in part because they quite clearly saw the way these churches underwrote corrupt and unjust ruling monarchies. To overthrow the monar-

---

in politics. See the discussion in Luke Bretherton, *Christ and the Common Life: Political Theology and the Case for Democracy* (Grand Rapids: Eerdmans, 2019), 256: "Secular philosophies . . . view religion as the enemy of forming a common life." My claim is that the values revolutions of the 1960s were/are perceived by many of their Christian critics as representing "secularism," or "secularization," understood popularly as a rejection of God and of biblical morality and therefore a marginalizing of Christianity and its moral values in culture.

chies would require attacking the church establishments that supported and legitimated them.

If we look at it that way, we must add another layer to our analysis. We must begin with the original authoritarian Christian regimes in such countries, whose corruptions and injustices helped trigger explicitly anti-Christian secular revolutions. These revolutions, in part because they were explicitly hostile to Christianity and the church, created their own religious resistance as well as movements toward counterrevolution whenever these became viable. These movements toward counterrevolution were often characterized by nostalgia for the lost Christendom regimes, despair over the damages perceived to have been wrought by secular revolutionaries, and a yearning for authoritarian Christian rulers. But the anti-religious impulses embedded on the "left" side of the politics of these nations also remained, and these too were often expressed in authoritarian ways by the state. Thus, a permanent dialectic of religious versus secular, conservative versus liberal/radical, and winner-take-all politics was created in nations like France and Russia and was available to be adapted and demagogued elsewhere. These are the original "culture wars."

In the next seven chapters, we will visit both first-wave and later-wave antidemocratic authoritarian reactionary Christianity. To prepare us for that, let's spend some time unpacking Walzer's argument to help us make sense of what we will encounter. In all the country studies that follow, we will attempt to offer both fair descriptions of the historical and political realities being considered, and some relevant applications to the problem of authoritarian reactionary Christianity in the United States and other lands today.

Post-War Secular Revolutions

The Paradox of Liberation addresses secular revolutions in the period of 1947–1962 and the religious counterrevolutions that followed. Walzer's case studies focus on Israel, India, and Algeria. He argues that in each case, the anti-colonial revolutionary movements that won national independence for these lands were intentionally and explicitly secular, and the revolutionaries sought to build secular cultures together with democratic politics. However, Walzer shows that before very long in each of these three countries power shifted to religious parties and movements.

The details differ, of course, and the differences matter. But Walzer summarizes the overall story in this striking quote:

> Initially, at least, this [national liberation] is a success story: the three nations were indeed liberated from foreign rule. At the same time, however, the states that now exist are not the states envisioned by the original leaders and intellectuals of the national liberation movements, and the moral/political culture of these states, their inner life, so to speak, is not at all what their founders expected. . . . [A]ll three movements were secular, committed, indeed, to an explicitly secular project, and yet in the states that they created a politics rooted in what we can loosely call fundamentalist religion is today very powerful. In three different countries, with three different religions, the timetable was remarkably similar: roughly twenty to thirty years after independence, the secular state was challenged by a militant religious movement.[3]

Early Zionism: A Secular Revolution

The most familiar case to me is the example of modern Israel. Its remarkable political and cultural evolution is worthy of extended consideration.

The modern Zionist movement was born in Europe in the late nineteenth century as an explicitly secular project. This movement rejected much of Jewish religiosity as it had developed over many

3. Walzer, *Paradox of Liberation*, xi–xii. Hereafter, page references will be given in parentheses in the text.

centuries of exile, persecution, and political homelessness within Christian Europe.

Walzer shows that the politics of Jewish life in the diaspora was a politics of "deference" to the gentiles and "deferred hope for divine redemption" (37). The early European Zionists argued that national independence for the Jewish people could only happen through the "negation of the exile" and an end to this diaspora Jewish political culture of deference and deferred hope, which had its rich dignity but in the view of the Zionists was not helpful for a modern nation-building project.

Because exilic Judaism had woven political theology, liturgy, and practice around this exilic experience, the Zionist project was understood to require "the creation of [Jewish] people who were hostile to Judaism . . . ending [exile] would be impossible without first 'negating' the cultural predispositions and habits, the mentality, of the exile" (38). In this sense, traditional Judaism would have to be sidelined for political Zionism to succeed in its goal of creating a modern Jewish state. It was quite a bold, even shocking, proposal, when one thinks about the sacredness, antiquity, and reach of the traditions that it was seeking to displace.

The Zionists, however, were serious about this vision. It predominated the nation-building efforts of the dominant Labor Party both before Israeli independence in 1948 and in the early years of newborn modern Israel. Labor Zionists sought to build a new country, modeled on the principles of the secular democratic politics of other nations—including, ironically, the Western European nations from which many Zionists had migrated (or fled). Meanwhile, they sought to build a culture of national pride, military service, physical vigor, attachment to the land through labor, equality between the sexes, engagement with the world, and an end to centuries of fear of and distance from non-Jews. To the extent that ancient Jewish religious sources were deemed relevant, it was the biblical "kings, warriors, and prophets" (45) that offered inspiration, not the tradition of pacific Torah and Talmud study under rabbinic leadership.

Followed by the Ultra-Orthodox Counterrevolution

Those who know the more recent history of Israel—or who visit it, as I have several times—are aware that the religious counterrevolution long ago arrived, in the form of "Israel's ultra-Orthodox Jews, the Haredim, the most rapidly growing sector of the population" (57). While the politics of the Haredim can take various forms, here is Walzer's biting analysis:

> [They] do not really think of the state as their own. Some of them are fierce nationalists . . . but they don't have the sense that citizens are supposed to have of being responsible for the whole; they don't recognize a "good" that is common to themselves and all other Israelis. They retain a view of the state typical of a stateless people, who are always outsiders, always vulnerable; they are political opportunists, seeking to seize whatever benefits the state provides and escape its burdens. The fellowship of democratic citizens and the freewheeling debates of democratic politics are largely alien to them; they participate in an older fellowship, accept as authoritative the rulings of their rabbis, and vote as a bloc. (57)

There is another wing to the recent religious counterrevolution, says Walzer. It is partly amalgamated with the Haredim vision and partly separate from it. This is found in the "messianic militancy" of the settler movement, a movement that grew in the period after the 1967 Arab-Israeli war. This war ended in a shocking Israeli military triumph that left Israel in control of the West Bank (including East Jerusalem) and Gaza Strip, a situation understood by the United Nations and almost the whole of the world community to be (at best) a temporary occupation of Palestinian land, subject to future peace negotiations.

After 1967, however, various Israeli governments began building settlements in these territories. Depending on who is doing the counting, there are around 400,000 settlers now living in the West Bank, with another 200,000 in East Jerusalem, in dozens of communities whose existence is fairly considered a violation of international law and of justice to a dominated Palestinian people. The settlers themselves are the vanguard of this project, the aggressive nature of which perhaps helps explain the peculiar sensibility that has developed among some of them. According to Walzer, "They are more than ready to use military force . . . a kind of thuggishness exists on the margins of the settler movement, tolerated and even encouraged by some of its central figures . . . nothing more clearly distinguishes the Judaism of the revival from the Judaism of the exile" (61).

Intensified by an End-Time Hope

One factor affecting both parts of the religious counterrevolution in modern Israel is the fact that, of course, modern Israel was built on the same revered Holy Land as is described in the ancient biblical texts. If "Israel" had been built in Uganda, as Zionist founder Theodor Herzl seriously considered, there would have been no religious resonance or territorial connection to ancient biblical faith.

It helps to remember that Israel in 1948 was established by the United Nations on land about half the size of modern-day Israel. Today's larger borders are the result of the 1948 war that resulted from the six nearby Arab nations' refusal to accept the UN decision. This, ironically, gave Israel a greater share of its ancient homeland. Then, after Israel's unexpected victory in the 1967 war, far more territory identified with ancient Israel came under modern Israel's control (though not international recognition). This included sacred territories with deep biblical resonances, especially the Old City of Jerusalem. After this it became even more plausible to see modern Israel as the fulfillment of eschatological hopes rather than just another newborn state in the post–World War II world. Modern statecraft in Israel became more vulnerable to giving way to ancient religion, ruling out political and diplomatic compromise, and blotting out the significance of local non-Jewish inhabitants, other than as foils for God's supposed redemptive plan.

In turn, modern democracy itself began to be questioned by some. Notes Walzer:

> For the settler militants, the nation-state as it exists today is simply an instrument for promoting God's politics—but not a very reliable instrument. They look forward to a time, as the editor of the settler magazine *Nekudah* argued more than a decade ago, when democracy (an alien Western form of government) will be replaced by an authentically Jewish religious regime that will lead Jews back to a life based on the Torah. (60)

An American Version of Religious Counterrevolution

Let us make the turn to our current moment in the United States and in other countries we will shortly discuss. Reading Walzer's account of secular revolutions and religious counterrevolutions, we cannot help but see the application and connection to today.

Many conservative Christians understand the social changes that erupted in the 1960s and have continued to this day as something like a secular revolution, whether an actual planned revolution (even a conspiracy) led by Christ's demonic and human enemies, or simply as a series of anti-Christian social movements. Powerful groups within conservative religious communities have been organizing explicitly for counterrevolution since the 1960s, and the narrative of cultural decline or secular revolution dominates many politically active conservative religious movements. The sense of embattlement, visceral reaction, and counterrevolutionary spirit has deepened over the last decade. Indeed, it is now sometimes explicitly part of movement vocabulary. I noted this in a recent article about the ultra-conservative Claremont Institute in California, where one leader, Glenn Elmers, has called for "all hands on deck as we enter the counterrevolutionary moment" and likewise stated that the 81 million Americans who voted for Joe Biden for president were "not Americans in any meaningful sense of the term."[4]

What if progress on the counterrevolution lags or meets reversals? Then, frustrated reactionary Christians tend toward a narrative of persecution, strategies of hunkering down or retreating from society—such as Rod Dreher's "Benedict Option"[5] and many similar proposals—and perhaps nurturing fantastical hopes of a coming apocalyptic divine intervention. But when their team notches victories, these same Christians exult in the victory of God and plan for further victories, because the counterrevolution is never over and there is always another enemy to defeat. This apocalyptic dynamic of counterrevolutionary despair and periodic jubilation is not conducive to healthy democratic politics. It has its own versions on the left, as well.

Whether in defeat or in victory, reactionary Christians pursuing their religious counterrevolution mainly appear to lack a political vision that—as Walzer notes in relation to Israeli politics—listens closely for the convictions or aspirations of those fellow citizens who do not share their religious vision. If God's victory means a dramatic loss of cherished freedoms for fellow citizens of different convictions, that is not a matter worth pausing over. The only vision of the common good held here is of the religio-moral counterrevolution that can save society.

Walzer's sketch of messianic militancy in Israeli politics, connected with retaking control of a land believed to be holy, leading to the possibility of imposing a conservative religious vision from

4. Elisabeth Zerofsky, "How the Claremont Institute Became a Nerve Center of the American Right," *New York Times Magazine*, August 3, 2022, https://tinyurl.com/msmbzenc.

5. Rod Dreher, *The Benedict Option: A Strategy for Christians in a Post-Christian Nation* (New York: Sentinel, 2017). Dreher has, tellingly, emerged from his retreat and is working on a different strategy right now. See chapter 9.

the center of political power, is highly relevant to authoritarian reactionary Christianity in many countries today. At least in modern Russia, Poland, and the United States, the idea of a special divine calling and relationship to these particular lands goes deep in the imagination of many believers. Certainly, in the United States, the idea of our nation as God's new chosen people and the vision of a full and thorough Christianizing of this sacred land go back to our earliest colonial era and are easily visible among many Christians today. Some of these same believers also embrace Christian Zionism, a conservative evangelical movement that treats Israel as Holy Land even today and draws specific anti-Palestinian policy consequences from this religious vision.

Taking a Nation Back for God by Any Means Necessary

Conservative Christian support for morally problematic leaders like, for example, Donald Trump and Vladimir Putin makes more sense within this framework of secular revolution and religious counterrevolution. Trump, for example, gained reactionary Christian support in large part because he sent every possible signal that he would wield his power relentlessly to achieve the religious counterrevolution that reactionary Christians have desired for so long.

This was not at all about Donald Trump's actual beliefs or character. It was about his promise to reactionary Christians that he would give them the political power needed to stage a religious counterrevolution, and his various claims suggesting that he would be its chief agent. In this sense, Trump delivered much of what he promised, as have other authoritarian reactionary Christian politicians whom we will consider here. That conviction has only been reinforced as Christians have witnessed and celebrated recent Supreme Court decisions. It also helps to explain the popular trope comparing Trump to the sixth-century BCE Persian emperor Cyrus, a biblical-era leader who advanced God's purposes despite not being a believer in the God of Israel.

It is a documented fact that the January 6, 2021, US Capitol insurrection and the preliminary efforts to overturn the 2020 presidential election contained a sizable conservative Christian presence, and had the acquiescence, "prayerful support," and fondest hopes of many Christians. This reveals the double-edged power of despair over the loss of a close election by their guy/their side, and a demonized reading of the Democratic Party that has swept through many conservative Christians.[6] It was a counterrevolutionary effort to win this battle once and for all. It also reveals at least a substantial fringe of reactionary Christians slipping free of the constraints of our democratic system and the rule of law.

When you are fighting a religious-cultural-ideological war for ultimate stakes, democracy is fine—*if you win.* But if you do not win, democracy may not be a matter of ultimate loyalty. Making sure your vision prevails may matter more. As Thomas Klingenstein, chairman of the board of the Claremont Institute, has put it: "If it's true that the country is as divided as we think it is, and if the situation is as dire, it's very important for conservatives to understand this. Because if you're actually in a war, even if it's a cold war, you behave differently. You're less inclined to compromise. You're more aggressive. In war, you don't negotiate until you've won."[7]

Is This Our *First* Religious Counterrevolution?

In the postscript to *The Paradox of Liberation*, Walzer addresses the question of whether the founding of the United States can be understood to offer yet another example of a secular liberation strug-

<hr/>

6. Consider these words from the 2022 Arizona Republican gubernatorial candidate Kari Lake: "It is not just a battle between Republicans and Democrats. This is a battle between freedom and tyranny, between authoritarianism and liberty and between good and evil." Robert Draper, "The Arizona Experiment," *New York Times Magazine*, August 21, 2022, 42.
7. Quoted in Zerofsky, "Claremont Institute."

gle followed by a religious counterrevolution—perhaps the Second Great Awakening of the early nineteenth century

His answer is that the comparison does not hold. The American Revolution established a secular state, but one that zealously protected religious freedom. Both religious and secular Americans came to see the benefits of this arrangement, considering the breadth of American religious diversity and the desire of people not to end up marginalized by some religious establishment or other. Meanwhile, since there was no single religious establishment against which this new arrangement was targeted, "the church" never had to become "the Enemy." America was "new" and "free," and together Americans arrived at a creative arrangement for public life, one that had never been attempted before.[8] That arrangement, embodied in the free exercise and disestablishment clauses of the First Amendment, has not been seriously challenged in American history, though the details of church/state and establishment/free exercise have been debated and litigated continually.

I believe it is now reasonable to suggest that the perceived secular revolution(s) of the 1960s finally created the motivation necessary for the United States to have its first experience of an organized religious (mainly Christian) counterrevolution. That counterrevolution is a force of such power that, for the first time in US history, it threatens not only the original "secular state with religious freedom" arrangements of 240 years ago but also American democracy itself.

One would not think that a stable political-religious democratic settlement sustained over more than two centuries would be sus-

8. The Frenchman Alexis de Tocqueville marveled at how, in the early United States, "Religious institutions have remained wholly distinct from political institutions, so that former laws have been easily changed whilst former belief has remained unshaken. Christianity has therefore retained a strong hold on the public mind in America." Alexis de Tocqueville, *Democracy in America* (New York: New American Library, 1956), part 2, book 1, 145. This classic work was originally published in 1835 and 1840.

ceptible to collapse in this way. Many of us Americans had come to take for granted that, at least here, there would be no such collapse. But when have any of us been assured of any human arrangement lasting forever?

A study of the history and current events in other countries, which we now begin, should forever disabuse us of such illusions. We will take a tour of seven countries where democracies have been weakened under the impact of authoritarian reactionary Christianity.

5

Reactionary Politics in France, 1870–1944

> What is the true nature of the French nation? Is it a
> collection of citizens, as the French Revolution would
> have it, or is it a large extended family huddled around
> its church, bound together by the cult of the dead and
> connected by ties of blood? It was undoubtedly this
> total form of nationalism, the nationalism of "blood
> and soil," that triumphed in the summer of 1940.
>
> —Zeev Sternhell (1986)[1]

A study of French political history is critical if one wants to understand the relationship between Christianity and democracy, as well as the grave difficulty of maintaining a stable democratic order, especially in an ideologically and religiously divided
society. Seeing the trouble that France has had in maintaining democracy over more than two centuries is instructive to those of us
in other democracies at risk of backsliding. Not being a French historian, I rely primarily here on someone who is: Frederick Brown,
author of *For the Soul of France* (2010) and *The Embrace of Unreason*
(2014).[2] The story that he tells is immensely relevant to the political
situation in the United States and other nations today.

1. Zeev Sternhell, *Neither Right nor Left: Fascist Ideology in France*,
trans. David Maisel (Princeton: Princeton University Press, 1986), xxxiii.
2. Frederick Brown, *For the Soul of France: Culture Wars in the Age of*

The Revolution Sweeps the Old (Catholic) Regime Aside

France before 1789 was governed by a conservative monarchy partnered with and supported by a conservative Catholic Church, though toleration of the Protestant minority had been extended by Louis XVI in 1787. The French term *ancien régime* (old regime) became widely used a few years after the French Revolution to name this medieval-type power structure composed of the Bourbon Dynasty, the broader aristocracy, and the church. Its perception by both the merchant class and the peasant masses as luxurious, repressive, and unresponsive to popular needs helped create the conditions for the French Revolution. As well, the Enlightenment ideals that had succeeded in driving the American Revolution had long circulated in France. These ideals were heightened in their significance by the success of the American Revolution, which the French government supported.

The French Revolution swept the *ancien régime* away—and did more than that. A movement that began under the influence of Enlightenment reason within a few years curdled into a bloodletting ever after known as the Reign of Terror. The French Revolution became the kind of revolutionary movement—not the last one, to be sure—that developed a dynamic of continuous radicalization, including an accelerating willingness to kill perceived counterrevolutionary enemies. Thus, France replaced a monarchical tyranny with a mob tyranny. This forever left its mark on French memory. The fact that only the soldier Napoleon Bonaparte was able to bring political stability to France, doing so by seizing power ten years after the revolution, also left its mark on the political memory of France. The French know in their bones the danger of both autocrat and mob.

The nineteenth century saw a dizzying political alternation in France between their first try at democracy, followed by the au-

---

Dreyfus (New York: Anchor Books, 2010), and *The Embrace of Unreason: France, 1914–1940* (New York: Anchor Books, 2014).

tocratic rule of Napoleon (1799–1814), then a return of the Bourbon monarchy (1814–1830, not counting an abortive effort by Napoleon to return to power in 1815), then a somewhat liberalizing constitutional monarchy under Louis Philippe I (1830–1848), then the birth of the Second Republic under Louis Napoleon Bonaparte (1848–1852), which evolved into the Second Empire when Louis Napoleon renamed himself Napoleon III (1852–1870). Finally the Third Republic emerged, born in 1870 after France lost to Prussia in the Franco-Prussian War. The Third Republic lasted till the birth of the collaborationist Vichy regime in 1940, which officially governed the country after the fall of France to the Nazis. France is today officially in its Fifth Republic period, which began in 1958. It has been a long and hard political journey.

The Bitter Culture Wars in France

By the late nineteenth century this political history had left France divided between royalists, Bonapartists, and republicans of various stripes. Moreover, during the Third Republic, Communism and socialism became major options. Indeed, Communism by this time had become an aggressive movement and a seemingly permanent force in world politics. Adding Communism (and its milder cousin socialism) to the existing political options on the left drove further bitter wedges into French politics. It also deepened the reactionary spirit of the French right wing.

The three primary right-wing figures of this period that Brown discusses in *The Embrace of Unreason* are the xenophobic, antisemitic, ultra-nationalist writer-politician Maurice Barrès (1862–1923); Charles Maurras (1868–1952), another writer-politician and founder of the pro-Catholic, royalist, periodically violent movement Action Française; and the more marginal figure Pierre Drieu La Rochelle (1893–1945). Drieu is most interesting for his wild transit through Communism to fascism to eventually becoming a leading pro-Nazi cultural figure in Paris during World War II. Maurras ended up in prison after a controversial trial for his actions during World War II. Drieu killed himself in disgrace in 1945.

We also meet other major figures who ended up in the French fascist orbit, including Jacques Doriot (1898-1945), Xavier Vallat (1891-1972), and Pierre Laval (1883-1945). Doriot, like Drieu a decorated veteran of World War I, founded the French Fascist Party in 1936, became a leading right-wing and antisemitic figure, and ended up being killed while serving Germany (not France) in February 1945. Vallat was a viciously antisemitic Catholic fascist who spent several years in jail for his role as commissioner of Jewish affairs in the collaborationist Vichy government, which sent thousands off to their deaths in Nazi camps. Laval, an older politician who had served as a prime minister in pre-war governments, became a high official in the Vichy regime, its most visible figure after its leader, the old war hero Marshall Philippe Pétain (1856-1951). Laval was executed in 1945 after the defeat of the Nazis and the collapse of Vichy.

Brown also discusses major figures on the Communist and Socialist left in the interwar period, tracing the increasingly intense, violent, and democratically unsustainable conflict between France's political left and right during the 1930s. Brown uses the slingshot movement *between* left and right of some key figures, such as Drieu, to illustrate the tendency toward the extremes in French politics during this period, marking the weakening of democracy as people sought salvation through extremist politics. This is always a warning sign in terms of the health of a democracy.

During the period we are considering here, parliamentary democracy in France, as in other countries, faced repeated body blows: World War I traumatization, unstable territorial changes, disputed national borders, economic misery, international tensions, ideologized gutter journalism, large refugee and migrant flows, the rise of paramilitary organizations on both right and left, and the weary public sense of democratic ineffectuality.

French Culture Warriors Welcome the Nazis

By the time the Nazis were ready to attack France in May 1940, the French were a politically weakened, divided, even exhausted nation. Rather than pulling together to face a grave foreign threat, they collapsed before the Nazi onslaught. Actually, it gets worse: part of the nation, including some of its most visible intellectual and political leaders, welcomed the Nazis.

This was not mainly a craven wartime surrender of conscience before the invader, as often happens in such situations. For some right-wing French people, the victory of the Nazis also marked the victory of their side in the French culture wars. These divisions dated back to the French Revolution but were profoundly exacerbated by the Dreyfus case of the 1890s. This case involved a French Jewish army officer who was falsely accused of treason, with evidence of his guilt invented, and evidence of his innocence concealed, by high officials in the French Army. Positions about the truthfulness of the accusations against Alfred Dreyfus became a frantically important point of division that ricocheted all through French society.[3] One might call the Dreyfus case the first Big Lie of modern Western politics.

The collaborationist Vichy regime in many ways incarnated the reactionary trends that had been developing on the right wing of French politics and culture. Vichy was certainly antidemocratic, antisemitic, and antiliberal, and it is generally described as paternalist, authoritarian, and reactionary-Catholic. It bears considerable responsibility for handing over more than 70,000 French and immigrant Jews to their Nazi murderers.

Historian Zeev Sternhell argues that Vichy marked a genuine ideological movement, a "national revolution" attempting to reverse the legacy of the French Revolution—a long-standing dream given

---

3. See both books by Frederick Brown, which treat the Dreyfus case at length.

unexpected opportunity by the circumstance of French defeat at Nazi hands:

> A serious ideological analysis of the national revolution leads necessarily to the conclusion that the Vichy regime undoubtedly carried out the ideological and political program found . . . [in] anti-Dreyfusism, in the work of Barrès and Maurras . . . it represented the revolt of an intellectual and political France that had never accepted the philosophy of ideological modernity . . . [and that] took the form of rebellion against liberal democracy.[4]

Authoritarian Reactionary Catholicism

Where was religion in all this? The story is complicated, but it can be summarized as follows. The Vatican, and the French Catholic authorities, licked their wounds over the French Revolution for well over a hundred years. Catholic losses during the Revolution were staggering, and the cultural changes that followed were most unwelcome. Decade after decade, the Catholic Church mainly functioned as a fiercely reactionary voice amid the maelstrom of French politics. It yearned for the *ancien régime* of which it had been such an important part. It said a repeated *non* to everything the French Revolution represented, really to everything the modern world represented: democracy, the separation of church and state, the liberalization of social values, and pluralism of all types.

Sadly, the French Catholic Church also tended to buy into the antisemitism that flourished in the late nineteenth century, as exemplified in the Dreyfus case. Jews became the symbol of all modern developments of which Catholic conservatives disapproved. (Protestants and Masons got their share of disapproval too.) Catholic media contributed amply to antisemitic discourse in France—

4. Sternhell, *Neither Right nor Left*, xxxv.

and not only in France.[5] Brown quotes this horrific Vatican diatribe from the era of the Dreyfus trial:

> The Jewish race, the deicide people, wandering throughout the world, brings with it everywhere the pestiferous breath of treason. And so too in the Dreyfus case . . . it is hardly surprising if we again find the Jew in the front ranks, or if we find that the betrayal of one's country has been Jewishly conspired and Jewishly executed.[6]

Overall, though there were notable modernists and various kinds of dissenters to reactionary French Catholicism, in the period we are considering the French Catholic Church positioned itself as a conservative partisan in the left/right culture wars rather than being able to rise above them with a more inclusive vision.

Incidentally, this was one reason for the broader failures of the Vatican during the rise of fascism in Europe.[7] Right-wing movements promised familiar conservative religious, social, and cultural goals, including the defeat of socialism, Communism, liberalism, internationalism, individualism, materialism, and the excesses of democracy. These goals were quite appealing to conservative Catholic officials, who echoed them in Vatican documents. The most famous of these was Pope Pius IX's now infamous 1864 "Syllabus of Errors,"[8] which offered a litany of antiliberal complaints.

The Catholic hierarchy was not able to arrive at a voice above left/right divisions, or a pro-democratic posture with constructive

5. David I. Kertzer, *The Popes against the Jews: The Vatican's Role in the Rise of Modern Anti-Semitism* (New York: Alfred A. Knopf, 2001).

6. Brown, *Soul of France*, 216.

7. There is a vast literature. Start with Michael Phayer, *The Catholic Church and the Holocaust, 1930–1965* (Bloomington: Indiana University Press, 2000).

8. The "Syllabus of Errors" was published as an appendix to the papal encyclical *Quanta Cura*. Accessed at https://tinyurl.com/4cws59vv.

engagement of various dimensions of modernity, until the church-wide Vatican Council II from 1962 to 1965. By this time, however, the Catholic Church had left a deep, and deeply discrediting, authoritarian and reactionary legacy.

They Sang the Old Songs without the Old Faith

Reactionary and eventually openly fascist voices like Barrès and Maurras sometimes had a tortured personal relationship with Christianity. They could sing the old songs but did not share the old faith—though Maurras converted to Catholicism just before his death. However, they shared with the Catholic Church nostalgia for the lost *ancien régime*, and their political preferences lined up very well with the Catholic hierarchy most of the time. Groups like Action Française were cobelligerents with the Catholic Church in the culture wars, evoking mixed theological-ethical reactions from the Catholic hierarchy but long periods of cooperation toward shared political goals.

Reading closely about figures like these offers a reminder that even thinkers and leaders who are post-Christian in their religious practice can articulate political ideologies that reflect the most reactionary tendencies of the churches they have left behind. Even worse, they often lack the moral scruples carried by some religionists who are just as reactionary in their politics but whose faith sets some boundaries on the politics they are willing to pursue.

Here is a telling example. In 1936, after yet another French politician had been driven to suicide by gutter journalism, Cardinal Liénart of Lille declared, "Politics does not justify everything," arguing that defamation and slander displease God, even if it is defamation and slander of *our* political enemies. But such religious scruples did not hinder others. Says Brown: "On the French Far Right, the will to destroy one's political adversary at all costs and by all means had replaced the conflict of ideas."[9]

9. Brown, *Embrace of Unreason*, 253.

One Thing Worse Than Christian Reactionary Politics

We see precisely this dynamic of irreligious conservative culture warriors in the US setting today. Young American conservative Nate Hochman, who wrote the brilliant piece on the irreligious right that we discussed in chapter 2, puts it this way: "The decline of organized religion on the right has, in fact, supercharged the culture war."[10]

The lesson for us may be that one thing worse than frankly Christian reactionary politics is its less scrupulous post-Christian, quasi-Christian, or corrupted Christian successor. Many US conservatives are as concerned as Cardinal Liénart was by the moral toxicity of the angrier strands of the American right, while also being readier than liberals are to see toxicity on the left as well. Conservative Christian American writer David French has written: "Our Christian political ethic is upside down. On a bipartisan basis, the church has formed its members to be *adamant* about policies that are difficult and contingent and *flexible* about virtues that are clear and mandatory."[11]

Those familiar with US politics might consider a comparison between the character, rhetoric, and policies of George W. Bush and those of Donald J. Trump, both Republican, both purportedly Christian, both supported by overwhelming numbers of white evangelical Christians. Bush proclaimed and at least initially attempted to practice a religious politics he called "compassionate conservatism." Trump did not. It is interesting to note that one of Trump's most amoral and dangerous advisors, Steve Bannon, according to multiple media reports, happens to be a fan of Charles Maurras.[12]

10. Nate Hochman, "The Doctrine of the Irreligious Right," *New York Times*, June 5, 2022, 5.

11. David French, "Christian Political Ethics Are Upside Down," *The Dispatch*, August 21, 2022, https://tinyurl.com/ypt66jvk.

12. Pema Levy, "Stephen Bannon Is a Fan of a French Philosopher . . . Who Was an Anti-Semite and a Nazi Supporter," *Mother Jones*, March 16, 2017, https://tinyurl.com/ms45bsax. For a bracing examination of Bannon, see Jennifer Senior, "American Rasputin," *Atlantic*, July/August 2022, 22–35.

Antidemocratic Energies in Long-Standing Democracies (Like Ours)

Today, on outward appearance, French politics is resolutely secular, and democracy seems stable. Religion is not widely practiced and the Catholic Church has little public role. However, as the *Economist* noted in November 2021, "France is seeing a disconcerting revival of ultranationalist thinking, and with it the rehabilitation of once-ostracized reactionary writers," like Charles Maurras.[13]

Right-wing figures, notably Marine Le Pen, have never won more votes in a post–World War II French presidential election than in the two rounds of the Spring 2022 election and the follow-up parliamentary elections of June 2022.[14] Reactionary, even arguably fascist voices, like Eric Zemmour, now inflamed by anti-Muslim sentiment along with earlier resentments, are increasingly significant in French politics.

Reactionary Catholic voices are among those surging. They have been increasingly visible since the *Manif pour tous* ("protest for everyone") movement of 2012–2013. According to journalist Harrison Stetler, these heavily Catholic, white, and mainly upper-crust protests were triggered by the French government's move to legalize same-sex marriage. Themes of an "eternal France" beset by forces of internal decadence (now what Zemmour calls "the LGBT lobby") and by threatening alien enemies (now mainly substituting Muslims for Jews) remind one of the painful political history we have been describing.[15]

France's long, difficult struggle with democracy, and with the relationship between democracy and Christianity, is instructive on many levels and for many other contexts. We learn that given the

---

13. "The Less Accused," *Economist*, November 20, 2021, 78–79.
14. "Jupiter Waning," *Economist*, June 25, 2022, 51–52.
15. Harrison Stetler, "Catholics for Zemmour," *Commonweal*, April 2022, 14–16.

right conditions, profoundly antidemocratic energies can emerge even in long-standing democracies. Where Christianity is involved, especially official church hierarchies that had once been aligned with the state, these antidemocratic energies come far more often from the right than from the left, and they tend to align with other reactionary forces in society. Nostalgia for the medieval world, for a lost Christendom, for authoritarian rule, for the marriage of throne and altar, for cultural uniformity grounded in shared Christian beliefs and values is a very powerful force. But it is a force that is bad for both the state and the church. As French philosopher Jean-Luc Marion has recently written, "When a religious community dies, it is almost always precisely because it committed the folly of letting itself be identified with a state, for states are mortal."[16]

Reactionary Christianity tends to harden where oppositional cultural voices seem most resolutely secular and anti-Christian in belief and in practice. France is one such example. The United States today seems like another.[17] In such contexts, it becomes difficult for mediating Christian theological and ethical voices to craft a path of conscientious partial accommodation to the modern world, a path that is both meaningfully Christian and meaningfully connected to today's world.[18] This is what I am trying to do in this book. Likewise, it seems more difficult for mediating voices from the secular side to craft a path of respectful engagement with their deeply religious fellow citizens. I honor those who attempt to do so.

16. Jean-Luc Marion, *A Brief Apology for a Catholic Moment*, trans. Stephen E. Lewis (Chicago: University of Chicago Press, 2021), 47.

17. Ross Douthat suggested this idea in his piece "Does Liberalism Need a Wolf at the Door?" *New York Times*, April 10, 2022, 9.

18. Two recent books describing, and offering, such mediating voices in France are Sarah Shortall, *Soldiers of God in a Secular World: Catholic Theology and Twentieth-Century French Politics* (Cambridge, MA: Harvard University Press, 2021), and Marion, *Brief Apology for a Catholic Moment*.

When such divides deepen, Christian leaders easily revert to a winner-take-all posture rather than being voices for civil peace through dialogue in the presence of profound differences. They are then opposed by resolutely secular forces who are just as scornful and just as committed to winner-take-all politics. It is a dangerous brew, inimical to the success of democracy.

6

The Politics of Cultural Despair in Germany, 1853–1933

> The conservative revolution was not a spontaneous
> or reactionary opposition to Versailles or to the Wei-
> mar Republic, but was the reformulation under
> more favorable historical conditions of a nineteenth-
> century ideology.

> —Fritz Stern (1961)[1]

Fritz Stern (1926–2016) came from an elite family of Jewish heritage who were forced to flee Nazi Germany for the United States in 1938. He eventually became University Professor at Columbia University and a distinguished historian of Germany. Stern will be our primary guide in this discussion of the most significant background ideological factors that contributed to the rise of Nazism in Germany. While the literature on late nineteenth-century and pre-Nazi Germany is voluminous, I choose Stern as our guide because I think his discussion is exceptionally germane to the matter of authoritarian reactionary Christian politics today.

1. Fritz Stern, *The Politics of Cultural Despair: A Study in the Rise of the Germanic Ideology* (Berkeley: University of California Press, 1961), 183.

Precursors to Hitler's Rise to Power

Stern's erudite 1961 book, *The Politics of Cultural Despair*, was a relatively early work demonstrating that Nazism was not simply a reaction to the German loss of World War I, the terms of the Versailles Treaty, or the failures of the democratic Weimar Republic (1919–1933). Instead, a proto-fascist ideology arose beginning in the mid-nineteenth century. It had some connections to similar right-wing movements elsewhere but also elements distinctive to German culture, history, and politics.

Through a close study of three successive figures—Paul de Lagarde (1827–1891), Julius Langbehn (1851–1907), and Arthur Moeller van den Bruck (1876–1925)—Stern shows that many elements that came to constitute Nazi ideology and even some policies were already in place many decades before Adolf Hitler rose to power. We will begin our study in 1853, as this was the date of Lagarde's first significant publication.

Stern calls this toxic configuration of longings and ideals "the Germanic ideology," though it has sometimes gone by other names: the *völkisch* movement, *Deutschtum*, or the "national conservative" movement. (It is a bit painful for one who knows this history to note that the same term, "national conservative" movement, is on the rise today in the United States.)[2] Stern's book title, *The Politics of Cultural Despair*, may capture the spirit of the movement more profoundly than any other label that he offers. His book profiles the three rather odd cultural critics who developed this vision, which under 1920s/1930s conditions was able to connect to angry masses of people and ultimately help usher the Nazi movement into power.

This terrible story reminds us, among other things, that ideas have consequences, and that one never knows when a ticking ideo-

---

2. See the National Conservatism website, for example: https://tinyurl.com/478h3bw3.

logical bomb will finally explode. It also has extraordinary relevance to today's authoritarian reactionary threats to democracy.

Three Alienated Intellectuals Set the Table

The picture that Fritz Stern paints of Lagarde, Langbehn, and Moeller van den Bruck is of brilliant but erratic intellectuals who, for reasons of background and temperament, felt alienated from established institutions in Germany. Lagarde was a biblical scholar focusing on ancient languages. Langbehn was an art historian. Moeller was a cultural historian who turned to political writing during and after World War I. None were trained political theorists. None served in government positions except military service. All three had difficult childhoods, felt deep distaste for modern Germany, and offered "reactionary-utopian" prescriptions for a better German future.

Reactionary-utopian: What does that mean? Consider these words from Lagarde: "The Germany that we love and that we yearn to see has never existed and perhaps never will exist."[3] The "Germanic ideology" which these three men helped to develop was backward-looking, in that it yearned for a lost Germany, or at least elements of an "ancient tradition" that supposedly existed in the mists of the past (Stern, xi). But it was also utopian, in that it dreamed of a future Germany that was not just better than the modern era, but better than any previous era. That makes little sense, but we are not in the realm of the rational here. Stern writes:

> The movement . . . sought to destroy the despised present in order to recapture an idealized past in an imaginary future. They were disinherited conservatives who had nothing to conserve, because the spiritual values of the past had largely been buried and the material remnants of conservative power did not interest them. They sought a breakthrough to the past and they

3. Stern, *Politics of Cultural Despair*, 27. Hereafter, page references will be given in parentheses in the text.

longed for a new community in which old ideas and institutions would once again command universal allegiance. (xvi)

These men were sharply negative in relation to their present, the period running from the mid-nineteenth century to the early 1920s. This era included the peasant-democratic, largely failed revolutions of 1848-1849, the defeat of France in the Franco-Prussian War (1870-1871), and the unification of Germany as an empire governed by King Wilhelm I and Prussian leader Otto von Bismarck and their successors beginning in 1871. Moeller van den Bruck also lived to see World War I (1914-1918), the loss of the war, the collapse of the Wilhelmine regime during the November Revolution of 1918, and the birth of the democratic Weimar Republic beginning in 1919.

Making Germany Great (Again)

But the political background seems less significant for these Germanic dreamers than it did for French figures like Barrès and Maurras. These figures did not so much yearn for a particular political order of the past as for a certain kind of German culture, which they uniformly believed to be eroding under the impact of modernity.

The culture that they disliked was, in their pessimistic view, urban, industrial, and capitalist; commercial, materialistic, and bourgeois; secular, rationalist, and scientific; bureaucratic, democratic, and mediocre; conflictual, pluralistic, and "Jewish." The main term used as a bogeyman to describe all these disliked characteristics was "liberal." This purported liberalism was causing Germany to lose its distinctive character and plunging it into a broader European mishmash, influenced by the French spirit of 1789. Anyone who sees the polemical uses to which that word "liberal" was subjected by these reactionary romantics recoils when the same strategies are used on the right today.

Lagarde, Langbehn, and Moeller painted a utopian picture of national rebirth in which all this awful liberalism would be left behind. Stern describes their ideology with the following characteristics:

Romantic "idealism." These men had little interest in real-world politics, or the choices made in everyday governance. They lived in a dream world, an imagined past and an idealized future. This mentality tended to make them unduly critical of current culture and unrealistic about the future. This dialectic between despair and utopianism became a breeding ground for political extremism, as it always does whenever it surfaces. Writes Stern: "They nurtured the idealistic rejection of modern society and the resentment against the imperfections of western ideals and institutions, that contributed so greatly to the debility of democracy in Germany" (xiv).

Blood and soil. Alienated by the rapid pace of German industrialization and urbanization, the Germanic ideologues identified the real Germany with its agrarian roots. The term *Blut und Boden*, "blood and soil," was coined in the late nineteenth century to name the purported mystical connection between the Germanic "race" and their land, and this romantic-agrarian concept later became central in Nazi ideology and policy. As Stern puts it: "They indulged in nostalgic recollections of the uncorrupted life of earlier rural communities, when men were peasants and kings true rulers" (xviii–xix).

Mystical nationalism and imperialism. The Germanic ideologues were firmly anti-internationalist and anti-European. They believed in the cultural superiority of Germany. They also were imperialists, not for reasons of realpolitik but in the same mystical way that they approached everything else. Lagarde believed that "a people can become a nation only through the collective acceptance of its divinely ordained mission." This God-given redemptive mission happened to be "the colonization of all non-German lands in the Austrian empire" (30).

Social unity. These men dreamed of a Germany unified, overcoming divisions of social class and identity, as well as long-standing regional and religious divisions. Social conflict violated their dreamy sense of how society should operate. Germany should be a unified social organism, not a squabbling chaos of conflicting groups and ideas. This is sometimes called an "organicist" understanding of politics. This vision of social unity has a recurrent appeal and surfaces frequently on the extreme left and right of politics.

Anti-Jewish politics. Of the three figures that Stern discusses, Lagarde was the most viciously antisemitic. Writing well before the end of the nineteenth century, he was already calling for the elimination of Jews from German life. He said that there was a worldwide Jewish conspiracy with the goal of world domination. He recycled the vicious and false antisemitic tropes that Jews controlled the press, higher education, law, medicine, entertainment, and capitalism. While he did not adopt the pseudoscientific racial version of antisemitism, he otherwise hit all the antisemitic themes of his era and the Nazi era that eventually followed.

Perhaps Lagarde's most atrocious written statement against the Jewish people was the following: "With trichinae and bacilli one does not negotiate, nor are [they] subjected to education: they are exterminated as quickly and as thoroughly as possible" (62–63). Lagarde was not the only writer making such statements in Germany or elsewhere in the late nineteenth century. But Stern offers ample evidence for the claim that "the ferocious Lagarde was the patron saint of the emergent anti-Semitic or *völkische* movement" in Germany (90). Societies in which groups of people are openly described in such dehumanizing language (of disease, vermin, animals) are ripe for violence, even for genocide. Those who care about healthy democratic politics will be very attentive to any surfacing of such language as, for example, Donald Trump deployed from the beginning of his presidential candidacy in 2015 when he attacked immigrants.

Strongman rule. The Germanic ideologues viewed democracy as an alien (mainly French) import to Germany that could not govern a great nation. They derided democracy and called for authoritarian leadership of some type.

They were not royalists. They did not look back longingly to monarchy. They were looking forward to a new emperor, a new Caesar, a new *Führer*—yes, they used the term that Hitler later adopted for himself. Lagarde wrote: "Only the pure, strong will of a Single Man can help us, a regal will, but not parliaments nor statutes nor the ambition of powerless individuals" (49). Stern comments: "Toward the end of his life, more and more insistently he called for a Führer who would so completely represent the people that in him they would be united and his command would be their will" (58). This is pure fascism, and wherever it arises it is fundamentally antithetical to democracy.

Christianity Meets Modernity: Old Certainties Shaken

The Germanic ideologues sought to create national spiritual unity in Germany through a new Germanic quasi-Christian religion. This theme is so central that we must linger over it here.

Germany, birthplace of the Reformation and center of the disastrous wars of religion, had no memory of Christian unity. Germany was late to arrive as a nation, and each region had its own unique history with the Protestant-Catholic split as well as with further Protestant sectarian differences. Prussia's foolish *Kulturkampf* of the 1870s—a war on Catholicism, led by the state under Bismarck—only exacerbated confessional divisions and weakened Christianity overall. There was no agreed German version of Christianity at the time these men lived. This helped to contribute to their desire for "a new faith, a new community of believers, a world of fixed standards and no doubts, a new national religion that would bind all Germans together" (xii).

Another factor contributing to the desire for a new faith, rather than a mere return to the past, was that already by the time of Lagarde, modern scholarship in religion had eroded Christian faith in important ways.

German biblical scholars had led the way in historical-critical study of the Bible. They were also the earliest leaders of the quest for the historical Jesus as opposed to simply accepting the canonical accounts. Naïve readings of the Bible were shredded among many, especially the intelligentsia.

German church historians were among the trailblazers in describing the historical factors that had led to the development of Christian creeds. It became much harder to view doctrine as something other than a human product.

German philosophers such as Ludwig Feuerbach were among the leading skeptics of Christian faith claims. The towering German philosopher Friedrich Nietzsche was among the first to proclaim that "God is dead"—that is, not just that the God in whom his pastor-father, church, and culture had believed never did exist, but that German culture itself was moving decisively away from such belief in God.

Stern shows that Lagarde was well ahead of Nietzsche: "A quarter of a century before Nietzsche's avowal that God is dead, Lagarde reported the spiritual bankruptcy of Christianity, proclaimed the death of religion in Germany and fulminated against the surface religiosity that had supplanted true faith" (38).

The weakening of Christianity's plausibility was frightening even to these men, who had themselves lost their faith. As Stern puts it: "The loss of religion heightened every other uncertainty, and they said—and often themselves felt—that life in the post-Christian, liberal era was unbearable" (xviii).

Germanic Quasi Christianity Fills the Vacuum

The reactionary figures we are considering believed that Germany could not do without a shared faith. But it would need to be "Germanic," nationalistic, and heroic, stripped of all Jewish elements, with a Jesus whom all "true Germans" could embrace. Lagarde, who was a biblical scholar and eventually was appointed to the religion faculty at Göttingen, appears to have been the primary pioneer of this new quasi-Christian faith. He was followed by numerous other distinguished professors who blazed the trail for a nazified faith.

First came the deconstructive work. Lagarde offered "an historical attack on the authenticity of [Christianity's] dogmas and a critique of its contemporary institutions. His aim was primarily negative: to clear away the rubble of the past and so prepare the ground for the building of a new national temple" (40).

Jesus would have to be rescued from Christianity, notably its Jewish elements. Stern describes the magnitude and supposed necessity of the task as viewed by Lagarde, who offered such atrocious and completely discredited biblical interpretations as the following:

> To divorce Christianity and Judaism even at this late stage would be a recognition of an unambiguous historical truth and of Jesus' own intent. He was not the Messiah of the Old Testament. This inspired mortal, this transcendent religious Genie of all human history, had in fact been a conscious rebel against Pharisaic Judaism. When Jesus said, "I am the Son of Man," he really meant . . . "I am not a Jew." The original act of rebellion should now be consummated, the Jewish past disavowed. (42)

Lagarde's critical vision also extended to the churches. He saw Protestantism as institutionally weak and uninspiring, a puny *Kulturreligion*. He saw Catholicism as un-Germanic but institutionally stronger and therefore more dangerous to Germany. He concluded that a wise German government would withdraw all institutional support from the existing churches to weaken them as much as possible (48). Hitler later found that seduction and intimidation worked better.

The "German Christian" Movement Takes the Baton

Lagarde's vision deeply appealed to the antisemites who followed him. It became important in the birth of the *Deutsche Christen* (DC) movement in the 1920s, for example. Those who study the relationship between Christianity and Nazi Germany always eventually find their way to the DC movement, which they usually first meet in 1933 when Protestant leaders like Karl Barth and Dietrich Bonhoeffer are battling its heresies in early Nazi Germany. The DCs were the ones most enthusiastically embracing Nazism and Hitler, happily supporting the nazification of the Protestant churches and working on stripping all "Jewish" elements out of church life.[4]

4. Consider Robert P. Ericksen and Susannah Heschel, eds., *Betrayal:*

This movement, it turns out, studied Lagarde deeply: "For some of the later nationalistic heresies, the German Christians [*Deutsche Christen*], for example, Lagarde became a patron saint. They regularly invoked him to justify their anti-Semitism, their blatant assertion that Jesus was an Aryan, their pagan brew of a Germanic faith" (42).

The DC movement liked Lagarde because he shared their agenda—indeed, he helped set it: Germanize Christianity, strip out all Jewish elements, take over or marginalize the existing churches, create a faith suitable for an ultranationalist, imperialist, authoritarian Germany. These movements "desire[d] to convert Christianity into a polemical, anti-Semitic, nationalistic faith and organization that would supplant the old and decadent tenets of a perverted and universal Christianity. In this distortion of Christianity and in the mass desertion from the Christian faith—one of the most obscure and most important aspects of the rise of national socialism—Lagarde's thought played a central role" (92).

Scholars of Nazi Germany have long known that quasi-Christian, sometimes frankly heretical, Christianity prevailed in large sections of Germany, and yet many Christian leaders and regular Christians in Germany supported it or at least tolerated it. This capitulation to a nazified Christianity has been a source of wonderment, but Stern's account helps us understand it.

Three Christian Paths to Nazified Quasi Christianity

Here is my summary of three paths toward apostate nazified quasi Christianity. I think these paths apply far beyond 1930s Germany.

German Churches and the Holocaust (Minneapolis: Augsburg Fortress, 1999); Richard Steigmann-Gall, *The Holy Reich: Nazi Conceptions of Christianity, 1919-1945* (Cambridge: Cambridge University Press, 2003); Karla Poewe, *New Religions and the Nazis* (New York: Routledge, 2006); Rainer Bucher, *Hitler's Theology: A Study in Political Religion*, trans. Rebecca Pohl (London: Continuum, 2011); Mary M. Solberg, *A Church Undone: Documents from the German Christian Faith Movement* (Minneapolis: Fortress, 2015).

Some Christians supported it because *they knew exactly what was going on and they fully embraced this "pagan brew"* of quasi-Christian Germanism. They went into DC/Lagarde-type quasi Christianity with their eyes wide open.

Other German Christians supported it or acquiesced to it because *they could no longer tell the difference* between Lagardian Germanic-pagan faith and historic confessional Christianity.

Finally, some Christians supported this toxic and dangerous faith because *they embraced the antiliberal politics that lay behind it.* Even if they saw certain problems with nazified theology or Nazi violence, the potential for political co-belligerency was too appetizing to pass up.

Overall, what Stern says of Lagarde, Langbehn, and Moeller has broad application:

> These men appealed to large segments of German society because they were idealistic and religious. For the Protestant academic classes had fused Christianity and German idealism so as to forge a *Kulturreligion*, which hid beneath pious allusions . . . a most thoroughgoing secularization. The religious *tone* remained, even after the religious faith and the religious canons had disappeared. . . . [They] appealed to the religious sentimentality of some, to the genuine desire for religion of others. (xxv)

Lagarde's ideas were especially toxic:

> He pushed the idea of a national rebirth from a Christian to a secular mystical meaning, down the treacherous slope toward the theology of politics. For his heroic program he invoked God's sanction, avowing that God's will and the Germanic religion coincided. By the 1920's, the idea of a national or racial rebirth had become a poisonous weapon . . . the more powerful for its religious ring. (50)

The result in Germany looked like this:

> Decades of political delusion had done their work, and many
> a conservative German shudderingly admired the terroristic
> idealism of Hitler's movement. The National Socialists gath-
> ered together the millions of malcontents, of whose existence
> the conservative revolutionaries had for so long spoken. (xxx)

In the end, the casualties included German democracy, international peace, and tens of millions of dead.

My contention is that authoritarian reactionary Christian
politics today in many lands also brings together political movements that offer a corrupted, quasi-Christian nationalist religion
bearing little resemblance to Jesus or historic Christian moral/
political norms.

For example, when one tunes in to some of the worship services
of the most ardent Trumpist pastors in America, quite often the anger, hyper-masculinism, and militant nationalism presented there
bear no resemblance to Jesus or historic Christianity. Something
debased and alien is going on. It ought to make the Christian's skin
crawl in intuitive recognition of its apostasy.

But these pastors, and the politicians alongside whom they have
debased Christianity, gain support from lots of ordinary Christians—because they embrace this debased faith, or don't recognize
it is debased, or acquiesce because they share its political goals—who
follow it right off the cliff.

7

Authoritarian Reactionary Christianity in Putin's Russia

> What is happening today in the field of international relations is . . . about human salvation, where humanity will be, on which side of God the Savior.
>
> —Patriarch Kirill, justifying Russia's 2022 invasion of Ukraine[1]

We begin our contemporary country studies with Russia, where Vladimir Putin's repressive, authoritarian police state justifies its draconian domestic and aggressive foreign policies in terms of reactionary Christian values, and with the full support of the leadership of the Russian Orthodox Church.

There can be no question that despite the outward appearance of democratic institutions, there is no democracy in Russia. After the collapse of the Soviet Union in 1991, it seemed for a happy moment that Russia might become a democracy. But in Russia the transition to democracy has been defeated under the autocratic rule of Vladimir Putin for the past two decades.

Russia is a personalist authoritarian state, ruled by one man

---

1. "Patriarchal Sermon in the Week of Cheese after the Liturgy in the Cathedral of Christ the Savior," March 6, 2022, https://tinyurl.com/bdfjfdvu.

with no current provision for a successor. There are no real elections, no free media, no independent judiciary, no political pluralism, no unhindered opposition leaders and parties. Civil society and human rights organizations have been hindered, harassed, or shuttered. Investigative journalists and opponents of the regime have been jailed and sometimes murdered, both inside and outside the country. All such repressive measures have intensified since the February 2022 invasion of Ukraine.

Freedom House (FH) classifies Russia as a "consolidated authoritarian regime," with an abysmal democracy score of just 5 out of 100 in its annual "Nations in Transit" report, released at the beginning of 2022.[2] That was before the invasion of Ukraine and the absolute ban on dissent against the war. This was FH's January 2022 topline summary of Russia's situation:

> With loyalist security forces, a subservient judiciary, a controlled media environment, and a legislature consisting of a ruling party and pliable opposition factions, the Kremlin is able to manipulate elections and suppress genuine dissent. Rampant corruption facilitates shifting links among state officials and organized crime groups.[3]

One-Man Rule Blessed by the Russian Orthodox Church

Vladimir Putin and his regime have received crucial support for their authoritarian rule from the Russian Orthodox Church, "now a fully assimilated part of the Kremlin's domestic and foreign policy machine," according to observers.[4] Putin justifies his repressive

---

2. "Nations in Transit 2022: Russia," Freedom House, https://tinyurl.com/yttkveat.

3. "Russia," Freedom House, https://tinyurl.com/3k4tf9mw.

4. Jeremy W. Lamoreaux and Lincoln Flake, "The Russian Orthodox Church, the Kremlin, and Religious (Il)liberalism in Russia," *Palgrave Communications* 4, no. 115 (2018), https://tinyurl.com/3yx4j6e3.

rule, in part, by claiming to be the defender of traditional Christian values, a posture that gains the support of the Russian Orthodox Church. Russia analysts Jeremy Lamoreaux and Lincoln Flake observe that "as early as 2000, when 'spiritual renewal' was highlighted in the National Security Concept as well as other government policies . . . Putin intended to cloak his regime in a type of Orthodox nationalism."[5] That strategy has only accelerated in the last two decades. Here is how the *Economist* summarized the situation in November 2021:

> Russia's securocrats assert that traditional values of family, culture and history are being corrupted by the liberal and licentious West and that only they can defend them. Fighting back against the West lets the Kremlin portray all those who oppose it—journalists, human rights lawyers and activists—as foreign agents.[6]

The trend was also noted in a 2018 article by religion scholar Chrissy Stroop in *Foreign Policy* magazine:

> Russia's new championing of so-called traditional values, such as homophobia and opposition to feminism and secularism, has received a powerful boost from the Orthodox Church—and from far-right fellow travelers in the West. . . . The ties between the Orthodox Church and the Russian state go all the way to the top. . . . Putin benefits from the backing of the Orthodox Church, an institution that, despite low levels of Russian piety and direct religious participation, enjoys considerable respect among the Russian people.[7]

5. Lamoreaux and Flake, "Russian Orthodox Church."

6. "Russia's New Era of Repression," *Economist*, November 13–19, 2021, 15, https://tinyurl.com/362xyeh7.

7. Chrissy Stroop, "Putin Wants God (or at Least the Church) on His Side," *Foreign Policy*, September 10, 2018, https://tinyurl.com/54fy4xyb.

Making Russia and Russian Orthodoxy Great Again

Stroop at the time already noted that Russian foreign policy adventurism has been underwritten by the Russian Orthodox hierarchy, vis-à-vis, most crucially, Ukraine. Here Russian imperialist, expansionist, or simply vengeful resentments and ambitions, together with the Russian Orthodox fight for preeminence in the Eastern Orthodox world, have led to a clear convergence of interests between the Putin regime and church leaders. Both wanted Ukraine subordinated to, if not absorbed by, Russia. Both considered the loss of control over Ukraine a blow to their interests and ideology. Both cooperated to subordinate Ukraine. This was clear long before the February 2022 invasion of Ukraine, which the Russian Orthodox patriarch Kirill was the world's only major religious leader to support.

In an infamous sermon on March 6, 2022, Patriarch Kirill treated the Russian military action as merely a response to a supposed Western attack on the Donbas region of Ukraine, claimed by Russia, on account of the faithful Orthodox region's unwillingness to host gay pride parades.

> Gay parades are designed to demonstrate that sin is one of the variations of human behavior. That's why in order to enter the club of those countries, it is necessary to hold a gay parade. . . . And we know how people resist these demands and how this resistance is suppressed by force. So it's about force imposing the sin condemned by God's law, and therefore by force imposing on people the denial of God and His truth. Therefore what is happening today in the field of international relations is . . . about human salvation, where humanity will be, on which side of God the Savior.[8]

Patriarch Kirill's argument should be taken seriously for what it reveals. He starts with the belief that homosexuality is a denial

8. "Patriarchal Sermon," https://tinyurl.com/bdfjfdvu.

of God, God's truth, and God's law. The good Orthodox people of the Donbas (supposedly) resisted the gay pride parades that mark the acceptance of this sin. Their resistance was (purportedly) suppressed by force—presumably, by the government of Ukraine. Russia is therefore contributing to human salvation by freeing the Donbas region from gay pride parades and the Orthodox believers from having to tolerate them.

In this sense, the invasion of Ukraine—understood by Putin to be a reclaiming of a part of greater Russia, in any case—is a contribution to God's work. If successful, it will also happen to (re)grow Russian territory and help make of Vladimir Putin a world-historical Russian leader akin to Peter the Great. If successful, it might not be his last such effort to claim more territory in his neighborhood.[9] This series of moves leverages homophobia by linking it to ultranationalism, imperialism, and the cult of strongman rule. It is a toxic combination.

Retooling a Thousand-Year-Old Dream

One term surfacing in media reports for the project Putin is undertaking is *Russkiy mir*—"The Russian world," a thousand-year-old concept recently retooled. In a March 2022 post, the *Economist* describes *Russkiy mir* as "a previously obscure historical term for a Slavic civilization based on shared ethnicity, religion and heritage. The Putin regime has revised, promulgated and debased this idea into an obscurantist anti-Western mixture of Orthodox dogma, nationalism, conspiracy theory and security-state Stalinism."[10]

---

9. Yaroslav Trofimov, "How Far Do Russia's Imperial Ambitions Go?" *Wall Street Journal*, June 25–26, 2022, C1. Mikhail Kasyanov, who served as Putin's prime minister from 2000 to 2004, is quoted in the article as follows: "If he is allowed to conquer some territories and Europe and the U.S. end up swallowing that fact, he will simply keep going forward."

10. "The Cult of War," *Economist*, March 26, 2022, 17–19.

Religion scholar John Burgess speaks of the Holy Rus' tradition, tracing it back to the conversion of Prince Vladimir in 988. Vladimir was converted to Byzantine Christianity through a visit to the Hagia Sophia in Constantinople. He brought the Orthodox faith back home. His "warriors and their families were baptized in the Dnieper River," in Kyiv. Orthodox Christianity became the point of unity for the tribes of the region and the cultures that developed there. Kyiv eventually fell to the Mongols. Constantinople was decimated by the Muslims in 1453. These developments "further strengthened Moscow's conviction that it had inherited the mantle of defender of true Christianity. The mythology of Moscow as the Third Rome [after Rome and Constantinople] was born."[11]

Out of these cultural elements, a renewed Holy Rus' dream appears to have emerged. This dream is of a reunited Slavic, or at least Russian-speaking, world, under the hegemony of Russia and characterized by traditional Russian Orthodox religion and moral values. Here Russia once again pitches itself as a defender of Christian civilization, but this time against the decadence of the Western liberal democracies. This project begins with Russia and territory to be reclaimed by Russia. Under the *Russkiy mir* label, it has been described by a former official of the Moscow Patriarchate as "the post-Soviet civil religion."[12] It is especially prominent in the Russian military and security services, as well as in the Orthodox hierarchy, and it is increasingly visible in the speeches of Putin himself.

While there is a distinctively Russian dimension to these themes, they also resonate elsewhere. An authoritarian male Christian head of government resolutely stands athwart history, sets his feet firmly in holy national soil, and resists left-liberal ideology in

11. John P. Burgess, "Orthodoxy and Identity," *Christian Century*, March 23, 2022, 10.

12. Francis X. Rocca, "'Russian World' Is the Civil Religion behind Putin's War," *Wall Street Journal*, March 19–20, 2022, C3.

order to defend not just one formerly Christian nation but Christian civilization itself. Homosexuality is taken to be the primary symbol of godless decadence that must be resisted. Democracy is sacrificed to this project, in part because Western liberal democracy is now understood to be a Trojan horse for godless left-liberalism, and in part because a Christian holy war to defeat the enemies of God is far more important. Various versions of this account animate the politics of every country we are considering in this book. Many millions of Christian people find such visions compelling.

The *Economist* describes Mr. Putin's mind-set since the invasion of Ukraine as follows:

> He is said to have lost much of his interest in current affairs and become preoccupied instead with history, paying particular heed to figures like Konstantin Leontyev, an ultra-reactionary 19th-century visionary who admired hierarchy and monarchy, cringed at democratic uniformity and believed in the freezing of time.[13]

Putin's hope for the war in Ukraine is not just to gobble up that country but "to wipe out the possibility of any future that looks toward Europe and some form of liberating modernity."[14] Putin's project is a textbook example of authoritarian reactionary Christian politics. It seems that for many Orthodox leaders and people in Russia, this is the politics that they now desire. Of course, given the repressiveness of Putin's regime, no one fully knows the state of public opinion in Russia. We do need to acknowledge the courageous statements of dissent from small numbers of Russians, secular and Orthodox. Such dissenters are now in prison. As the war against Ukraine has continued, with serious setbacks and massive loss of life on both sides, public evidence of dissent on the part of

13. "The Cult of War," 19.
14. "The Cult of War," 19.

Russian people has grown, and many tens of thousands have fled the country. Still, at least for many Russian Christians over the last two decades, if the choice has been between the authoritarian reactionary Christian regime of Vladimir Putin, with all that entails, and constitutional democracy with political rights, civil liberties, and genuine rule of law, these Christians have chosen the former—with disastrous consequences.

8

Authoritarian Reactionary Christianity in the Recent Politics of Poland

> The Polish PiS [Law and Justice] government is still succeeding in presenting itself as both the protector of the Catholic Church and the defender of the national identity.
>
> —Astrid Prange (2017)[1]

L et us now turn to the case of Poland, classified as a "semi-consolidated democracy" in Freedom House's most recent nations-in-transit report, which gives Poland a current democracy score of 59 out of 100, down from 65 just two year earlier, marking its sixth consecutive year of decline.[2] In the period from 2015 to 2021, under the Law and Justice (PiS) party, Poland clashed frequently with the European Union (EU), other member states, and EU legal bodies, related to Polish government actions found to be in violation of EU laws and human rights standards. The concerns were sufficiently serious that the EU froze $40 billion in pandemic-

---

1. Astrid Prange, "Of Popes and Politicians," *Deutsche Welle*, July 24, 2017, https://tinyurl.com/2kt7cusu.
2. "Nations in Transit 2022: Poland," Freedom House, https://tinyurl.com/mjs4xupu.

recovery funds set aside for Poland, which in turn evoked outraged claims that Poland was being punished arbitrarily and unfairly.

The government, in turn, attempted to score domestic political points out of its conflicts with the EU, with one major official even threatening to withdraw Poland from the EU. If the writing of Polish politician-philosopher Ryszard Legutko is any indication, at least part of the conservative constituency in Poland believes that the EU is importing left-liberalism in the name of liberal democracy, and that submitting to its dictates on cultural matters is what is truly undemocratic.[3]

It should be noted that the major opposition party in Poland, the Civic Platform, which led Poland from 2007 to 2014, is very much a liberal-minded pro-European Union party. The divisions between Civic Platform and Law and Justice, and the people attracted to each, are both very deep and very similar to partisan-ideological divisions in the United States. That itself is very striking because the histories of these two countries are so different. It seems that the left/right religious and ethical divisions we are considering are more significant than national histories, especially in a globalized social media context in which ideas jump borders instantaneously.

The Russian invasion of Ukraine in February 2022, and the decision of the United States and NATO to resist it by all means short of direct military intervention, has dramatically changed the political situation in Poland, signaling new possibilities for the direction of Polish politics. It has also begun a rapid thaw in relations between Poland and the EU, both of which confront a disturbing set of economic, energy, and security challenges that they need to face together.

---

3. Ryszard Legutko, *The Demon in Democracy: Totalitarian Temptations in Free Societies*, trans. Teresa Adelson (New York: Encounter Books, 2018), 58–65. His perspective is shared by American conservative writer Christopher Caldwell, "Poland against the Progressives," *Claremont Review of Books*, Winter 2021/2022, 34–39.

Democratic Backsliding in Poland

It remains relevant to consider the recent politics of Poland for any lessons it might offer related to authoritarian reactionary Christian politics. In its most recent report, posted in early 2022 before the Russian attack on Ukraine (but after other Russian incursions into Ukraine), Freedom House summarizes the health of democracy in Poland as follows:

> Poland's democratic institutions took root at the start of its transition from communist rule in 1989. Rapid economic growth and other societal changes have benefited some segments of the population more than others, contributing to a deep divide between liberal, pro-European parties and those purporting to defend national interests and "traditional" Polish Catholic values. Since taking power in late 2015, a coalition led by the populist, socially conservative Law and Justice (PiS) party has enacted numerous measures that have increased political influence over state institutions and damaged Poland's democratic progress. Recent years have seen an increase in nationalist, homophobic, and discriminatory rhetoric.[4]

Poland's recent backsliding from democratic norms is especially striking given its zealous role in advancing democracy in Eastern Europe in the post-Soviet era. Indeed, as international-relations scholars Tsveta Petrova and Senem Aydin-Düzgit have argued:

> Polish support for democracy in its region had already begun in the 1980s. The Polish anti-communist movement Solidarity carried out activities to mobilize and assist allies in other countries fighting against the Soviet system. Some of these activists later laid the ideological and organizational foundations of civil

---

4. "Poland," Freedom House, https://tinyurl.com/33n6zsmt.

society in post-communist Poland, resulting in the establishment of a number of civic organizations that developed ambitious international democracy assistance efforts.[5]

But a country that had embraced democratization so ardently, and even evangelistically, has been moving backward, at least according to Freedom House democratic-norms standards.[6] These begin with the regime's unwillingness to administer a fully fair presidential election in 2021. For example, public broadcasting was mobilized to support the government's candidates, and the Organization for Security and Co-operation in Europe (OSCE) found that the rhetoric on regime-dominated public broadcasting was "xenophobic, homophobic, and antisemitic." (British and US readers might consider the significance of the independence and restraint of the BBC and National Public Radio by comparison, and also note the attacks on these media outlets from the right.) Government funds were also deployed to support candidates of the ruling coalition rather than all candidates. Public funds in Poland at this time are disproportionately directed to civil society organizations and local municipalities sympathetic to the current conservative government, and the freedom of assembly of pro-regime groups is privileged over that of other groups.

Not only has public media independence been compromised, but there have been declines in the independence of the private media sector. This includes the purchase by a state-owned gas company of Polska Press, which owns over 80 percent of the largest Polish regional newspapers, which puts the current government in charge of most media in the country. "Strategic lawsuits against public participation" (SLAPPs) have been deployed to intimidate and

5. Tsveta Petrova and Senem Aydin-Düzgit, "Democracy Support without Democracy: The Cases of Turkey and Poland," Carnegie Endowment for International Peace, January 5, 2021, https://tinyurl.com/6mt2zuhb.

6. "Freedom in the World 2022: Poland," Freedom House, https://tinyurl.com/m53ma57j.

harass journalists, private media has been threatened with heavy tax burdens, and there have been reports of government intimidation and some physical attacks on journalists.

Another major issue has been what Freedom House calls the "instrumentalization" of the nation's Constitutional Tribunal to make abortion law much more restrictive. Judicial independence has been weakened on multiple fronts, including through a "muzzle law" banning judges from criticizing the government. No area is more contested in the politics of contemporary Poland than the judiciary, which is viewed as captured by left-liberalism by conservatives and as a bulwark of rule-of-law by the liberals.

Journalist/historian Anne Applebaum holds Polish citizenship and is married to Radoslaw Sikorski, who served as Poland's defense minister and foreign minister and is a member of the European Parliament. Applebaum has described the governing Law and Justice Party, led by Jarosław Kaczyński, as "not just xenophobic and paranoid but openly authoritarian." To the concerns articulated by Freedom House she adds the gutting of the civil service, diplomatic corps, and military; the government and state media's descent into blatant falsehoods; attacks on individuals and conspiracy theories; and the return of public antisemitism.[7]

Finally, local and regional governments have passed anti-LGBTQ+ resolutions, and the federal parliament considered legislation that would ban outright any pro-LGBTQ+ public demonstrations. Anti-gay rhetoric is rampant on the conservative side of public life. And this leads me to a story.

The Mainstreaming of Homophobia in the Name of Freedom

Ryszard Legutko is a significant conservative intellectual and political voice in Poland. He teaches philosophy at Jagiellonian Univer-

---

7. Anne Applebaum, *Twilight of Democracy: The Seductive Lure of Authoritarianism* (New York: Anchor Books, 2021), 4–11.

sity and has written learned studies on the Greek philosophers and on democratic theory. He served as minister of education and secretary of state in the government of the late president Lech Kaczyński, who was the brother of Jarosław, and with him cofounded the Law and Justice Party. Legutko served as deputy speaker of the Polish Senate and is currently a member of the European Parliament. His book *The Demon in Democracy* is highly influential in the international conservative conversation. His scheduled invitation from a student group to speak at Middlebury College in 2019 was cancelled under pressure, which made Legutko yet another distinguished conservative "victim" of left-liberal "cancel culture."[8]

In *Demon in Democracy*, Legutko compares what he describes as the stifling power of liberal language-policing to Communist totalitarianism. Liberal language-policing is a real thing—this is to be admitted. But there are reasons why language matters. To make his point, Legutko offers multiple examples associated with homosexuality. As he does so he uses a shocking term of contempt for LGBTQ+ people that I am unwilling to print in full here, as it is a weapon deployed to demean vulnerable people all over the world and often is accompanied by violence against them. Anti-gay slurs ought to be condemned, as are all other terms of contempt hurled at out-groups. Language matters because words are essential to human life and language is a part of how we treat people. Hostile and inflammatory public language from influential people especially matters because it has the repeatedly documented power to direct harm toward its targets.

Here is an example of what Legutko does with his anti-gay slurs. He seems to be trying to make an argument against liberal language patrolling, but how it reads is as a further attack on gay people:

8. Riley Board, "College Braces for Right-Wing Speaker Accused of Homophobia," *Middlebury Campus*, April 16, 2019, https://tinyurl.com/ypdps8dd. See also Molly Walsh, "Middlebury College Cancels Forum Featuring Conservative Polish Leader," *Seven Days Vermont*, April 17, 2019, https://tinyurl.com/29tshhcx.

Language was the first to go down this road: initially thought of as potentially descriptive and neutral, it soon came to be seen as the major political weapon used by the oppressors against the oppressed. Thus the f****t jokes are not harmless anecdotes, sometimes funny and sometimes not: the mere fact of using the word "f****t" in speech, public or private, is an act of participation in the exclusion of homosexuals from the democratic cooperation . . . [a] thought-crime, a mental sin that constitutes the first act of disobedience to holy political principles.[9]

Left-liberalism is the new orthodoxy, this new orthodoxy must be rejected, and one way to do this is to offer anti-gay slurs in print.

Legutko's book offers a robust statement in defense of traditional Polish Catholic culture, religion, and moral values, which he demands be treated respectfully and that he says are under assault by EU left-liberal orthodoxy. On its face these are claims to be taken seriously. But dehumanizing slurs are unchristian, immoral, and dangerous. It is very hard to look with sympathy upon those who integrate such slurs into their defense of "Christian civilization." I say this precisely as a serious Christian. It is difficult not to conclude that there is much that is unholy within authoritarian reactionary Christianity.

Conservative Catholic Support for Law and Justice Party

The Law and Justice Party, which Legutko has served, gains the bulk of its support from conservative Catholics as well as a warm relationship with the Polish Catholic leadership. This situation was summarized in a Summer 2017 article by *Deutsche Welle* reporter Astrid Prange:

Poland as the "bulwark of Christianity" . . . [is] an outlook the Polish Bishops' Conference and the PiS [Law and Justice] govern-

9. Legutko, *Demon in Democracy*, 100, 101.

ment have in common. They feel they must defend themselves as much against the secularization of the West as against the supposed proliferation of Islam. The Polish PiS government is still succeeding in presenting itself as both the protector of the Catholic Church and the defender of the national identity.[10]

Prange and other observers have noted that numerous Catholic clergy in Poland have openly urged their people to vote for the Law and Justice Party, even though this violates the official agreement on the church-state relationship in Poland.[11] This is a common move in authoritarian reactionary Christianity, and almost always a very bad idea. It identifies Jesus and Christianity with a worldly political party, and in polarized contexts damages the church's appeal to all who don't share that party's politics. Some clergy have also descended to crude anti-gay rhetoric such as when the archbishop of Krakow described homosexuals as "a rainbow-colored 'plague' that had replaced the 'red plague' of Communism."[12] Law and Justice and other conservative parties have deployed such inflammatory rhetoric both to get out the vote and to consolidate church support.

John Paul II and Democracy in Poland

The intertwining of national and religious identity in Poland helped to provide that nation the strength to survive decades of foreign domination, even periods when a nation called Poland had been erased from the map. All students of John Paul II, the only Polish pope and one of the most significant religious leaders of the twentieth century, know that his powerful evocation of Polish Catholic

10. Astrid Prange, "Of Popes and Politicians," *Deutsche Welle*, July 24, 2017, https://tinyurl.com/2kt7cusu.

11. Justyna Pawlak and Alicja Ptak, "As Poland's Church Embraces Politics, Catholics Depart," Reuters, February 3, 2021, https://tinyurl.com/24bjn7de.

12. Applebaum, *Twilight of Democracy*, 7.

identity and values was crucial not just in resisting Communist domination in Poland but eventually in bringing about its collapse. The historical connection between Catholicism and historic Polish identity certainly appears to parallel the similarly powerful connection between Orthodoxy and Russian identity.

These are facts, and on their own these facts are not problematic. But the current governing coalition in Poland has in recent years offered a troubling example of antidemocratic authoritarian tendencies advancing in partnership with conservative Christianity, in this case Catholicism. This was not part of John Paul II's agenda and must not be identified with it.

Russia, sadly, never consolidated a democracy after the fall of Communism and the breakup of the Soviet Union. But Poland did do so. It joined NATO and the European Union, and it built an impressive democracy. Poland has backslid in terms of some democratic norms, and its semi-deconsolidation is intertwined with conservative Catholicism and supported by both grassroots and leadership Catholics. It has also flirted openly with antisemitism, a substantial problem in Polish history (as throughout Europe) and deeply painful in the land where three million Polish Jews, and many non-Polish Jews, were murdered by the Nazis during World War II.

The Polish government and people are to be applauded for the gracious and sacrificial way they have opened their arms to Ukrainian war refugees, now numbering over four million—more than any other country has taken in. Poland has also supported and helped transit weapons flows across its territory to Ukraine in its existential effort to defend itself. The Russian invasion of Ukraine gravely threatens Poland as well, and the Poles knew and declared that Vladimir Putin's Russia was dangerous long before most other European countries saw the situation clearly.[13] All of

13. "The Poles' Position," *Economist*, July 2, 2022, 47.

this has created a new context for relations between Poland, the European Union, and the United States. It may also have reminded the Polish government and people of the dangers of authoritarian politics, Christian or otherwise. I hope for a better future for Poland than that represented by authoritarian reactionary Christianity.

9

Authoritarian Reactionary Christianity in Orbán's Hungary

Orbán's embrace of religion has served to consolidate his power, "other" his opponents and shield Hungary from EU criticism of its attacks on the rule of law. . . . It is . . . a dangerous model for how religion can be used to fuel democratic backsliding.

—Carolyn Gallaher and Garret Martin (2020)[1]

Hungary arguably offers the most disturbing example of democratic backsliding in Europe. What makes it even more disturbing is the influence that nation's authoritarian reactionary Christian paradigm is having well beyond its borders. Far more than Russia, especially since the 2022 invasion of Ukraine, Hungary is providing both the ideas and the example for reactionary Christian politics all over the world, perhaps especially in the United States.[2]

1. Carolyn Gallaher and Garret Martin, "Viktor Orbán's Use and Misuse of Religion Serves as a Warning to Western Democracies," American University, October 27, 2020, https://tinyurl.com/3tywskww.
2. Andrew Marantz, "The Illiberal Order," *Atlantic*, July 4, 2022, 36–47.

Viktor Orbán and "Illiberal Democracy"

Hungary is classified as a transitional or hybrid regime (that is, between democracy and autocracy) in Freedom House's most recent nations-in-transit report, with a score of 45 out of 100. Here is the topline summary from FH on Hungary:

> After taking power in the 2010 elections, Prime Minister Viktor Orbán's Alliance of Young Democrats–Hungarian Civic Union (Fidesz) party pushed through constitutional and legal changes that have allowed it to consolidate control over the country's independent institutions, including the judiciary. The Fidesz government has since passed antimigrant and anti-LGBT+ policies, as well as laws that hamper the operations of opposition groups, journalists, universities, and nongovernmental organizations (NGOs) that are critical of the ruling party or whose perspectives Fidesz otherwise finds unfavorable.[3]

Hungary is ruled with ingenious authoritarianism by Viktor Orbán, one of the most remarkable political figures of our time. Orbán, born in 1963, began his rise to prominence when he served as leader of a pro-democratic student movement in Communist Hungary. After Communism collapsed, he was elected to parliament at twenty-seven as the head of the new Fidesz party. Fidesz was an acronym for Alliance of Young Democrats, and at its inception it was a pro-European center-right party that indeed supported the principles of liberal democracy. As head of Fidesz, Orbán served as prime minister from 1998 to 2002. After his bitterly disappointing defeat in 2002, he led the Fidesz party in opposition. Coming to power again in 2010, he has moved his party and his nation sharply toward rightwing populism of an authoritarian reactionary Christian type. In 2014, Orbán for the first time described his vision of Hungary's fu-

---

3. "Hungary," Freedom House, https://tinyurl.com/5dxt6s8c.

ture as an "illiberal state."[4] More often today his governing model is described as "illiberal democracy," but what he is doing violates democratic norms so clearly that it is hard to see why it should be given any version of the term "democracy." In any case, that label—illiberal democracy—and Orbán's example have electrified authoritarian conservatives all around the world, providing a blueprint for the dismantling of a democracy in relatively short order.

Rigging the Rules of Democracy

Today, Orbán's Fidesz party together with the Christian Democratic People's Party controls a supermajority in parliament and dominates every branch, and pretty much every function, of Hungarian government. It is hard to know where to begin in documenting the autocratic moves that Orbán's government has undertaken.

We will start with elections. As in Poland, Freedom House judges Hungary's elections as free but not fair. Besides ruthless gerrymandering, the government dominates public media and directs public funds to support party candidates. In the recent April 3, 2022, election, Orbán won with 53 percent of the vote, despite a concerted effort by the opposition to unite in order to drive him from office before he settles in for life.

The *Economist* suggests that Orbán was able to win again in part by leveraging the Russian invasion of Ukraine through the relentless use and abuse of state media, which "relayed his baseless claim that the opposition would drag Hungary into war with Russia."[5] But the election was by no means fair. The *Washington Post* summarized the three primary reasons for Orbán's win as "rigged rules, a horrible war, and autocratic cheating."[6] The rigged system is apparent

4. Zsuzsanna Szelényi, "How Viktor Orbán Built His Illiberal State," *New Republic*, April 5, 2022, https://tinyurl.com/4hd6kmcs.
5. "Vaccinated against Viktor," *Economist*, April 9, 2022, 42.
6. Kim Lane Scheppele, "In Hungary, Orbán Wins Again—Because He

in the fact that winning a mere 53 percent of the vote got him 83 percent of the districts and thus total domination in parliament. Also notice this little electoral innovation:

> A November law introduced "voter tourism," allowing any Hungarian citizen to legally register to vote in any district. Before the election, evidence surfaced that voters were being strategically moved into districts that might otherwise be close, with hundreds of voters registered at single residences. On Election Day, monitors documented minibuses delivering clusters of voters to polls.[7]

A Degraded Judiciary and a War Against LGBTQ+ People

Hungary has also witnessed disturbing losses for judicial independence. Media independence and pluralism have likewise been compromised. Corruption and nepotism, heading in the direction of a classic kleptocratic state, have become obvious. Public universities are being privatized and taken over by private asset-management foundations led by pro-government figures. The government is directing which programs can and cannot be taught (for example, by eliminating gender studies programs for ideological reasons).[8] NGOs have been harassed, at the prime minister's instigation, for years.[9] The vastly powerful Pegasus spyware program out of the NSO company in Israel has been used by the government for surveillance of political opponents, journalists, civil society leaders, and many others.[10]

Has Rigged the System," *Washington Post*, April 7, 2022, https://tinyurl.com/bdh5s2nd.

7. Scheppele, "Orbán Wins Again."

8. Elizabeth Redden, "Hungary Officially Ends Gender Studies Programs," *Inside Higher Ed*, October 17, 2018, https://tinyurl.com/3a25vbu6.

9. Hungarian Civil Liberties Union, "Harassment of NGOs Was Ordered by Hungarian Prime Minister," *Liberties*, October 10, 2016, https://tinyurl.com/yn3dzv9x.

10. Shaun Walker, "Hungarian Journalists Targeted with Pegasus

In short, it appears that if there is a way for the regime to centralize power and weaken independent thought and democratic oversight, Orbán finds it. This is autocratic rule with tremendous shrewdness and full awareness of the many nodes of political and governmental power that must be first neutralized, then seized, and finally weaponized.

Anti-LGBTQ+ agitation, directly from the central government in Budapest, is aggressive and brutal. An "anti-pedophile" law was passed in 2021 as yet another way of demonizing sexual minorities, this time by the old trope linking them spuriously to the abuse of children.[11] Freedom House describes the Hungarian government under Orbán as waging "ideological war" on LGBTQ+ people. More broadly, "increasing lack of respect for vulnerable groups" targeted by government rhetoric has created a hostile and even dangerous environment for many.

Hungary has continued its role as the most Russia-friendly NATO and EU country, even since the invasion. This has isolated it from some of its former allies in the eastern part of the EU, including Poland, while perhaps protecting it from Russia's wrath.[12] And, while Poland is patching up its relationship with the EU and regaining full access to EU funds, Hungary is not, and its financial losses as EU punishment for Orbán's democratic backsliding will be substantial. But all such losses will be used as antiliberal propaganda for the regime.

Orbán Becomes a Global Christian Superstar

Viktor Orbán has become a model, even a hero, of the US American right. *New York Times* writer Elisabeth Zerofsky reports that there

---

Spyware to Sue State," *Guardian*, January 28, 2022, https://tinyurl.com/5da25paz.

11. Rita Beres-Deak, "What Is the Hungarian 'Pedophilia Act' and What Is Behind It?" *Lefteast*, June 16, 2021, https://tinyurl.com/3yvuay9s.

12. Giorgio Cafiero, "Analysis: Ukraine War Has Both Blindsided and Empowered Orban," *Al Jazeera*, June 27, 2022, https://tinyurl.com/kj7aay7r.

is no more influential figure abroad in influencing the direction and the strategy of the American right, and her reporting shows exactly how many conservatives are making the pilgrimage to Budapest.[13] Fox News star Tucker Carlson visited Orbán in Budapest in 2021, spending a week celebrating him on his influential evening program. This unprecedented step by Carlson offered a major boost to Orbán's visibility among American conservatives.

In her October 2021 piece, Zerofsky describes her talks with celebrated Christian conservative Rod Dreher, with whom she visited while he was being hosted in Budapest on a Danube Institute fellowship. In a piece posted ten months later, Andrew Marantz interviewed Dreher, who was still in Budapest and attending the American Conservative Union's Conservative Political Action Conference of May 2022, a CPAC event being hosted in Europe for the first time ever. Marantz quotes Dreher as saying that what the Republican Party needs now is "a leader with Orbán's vision," a new "American Orbánism." We also learn the startling news that Dreher is so smitten that he is considering relocating permanently to Budapest, where he has been offered a job by the government-funded Danube Institute. Says Dreher: "There are many things that the Americans here want to learn from the Hungarians. We're going to keep our heritage for ourselves, our Christian heritage, our ethnic heritage . . . that's what I think they want to say but can't say, and so they point to someone who can say it." Marantz concludes: "Dreher had completed his transition from aspiring ascetic to partisan booster."[14]

The hits kept coming for Orbán. He next was the star speaker at the US Conservative Political Action Conference in Dallas in August 2022. This was not long after making headlines for a speech in which he decried immigration as making nations into mere "conglomeration[s] of peoples" and said that "we do not want to become

---

13. Elisabeth Zerofsky, "The Orbán Effect," *New York Times Magazine*, October 24, 2021, 22–29.

14. Marantz, "Illiberal Order," 42, 46–47.

peoples of mixed-race."[15] This did not disqualify him from addressing CPAC or receiving the warmest of receptions.

Duped by Religious Rhetoric (Again)

Viktor Orbán's explicit "illiberal democracy" agenda has been repeatedly defended by him as a Christian project, with many Christians thrilled about what he is doing. American University professors Carolyn Gallaher and Garret Martin, in an October 2020 post, say this:

> Orbán has, up to now, skillfully taken advantage of the EU's divisions and weaknesses to avoid any major consequences for his country's democratic backsliding. He has conveniently used Christianity as a shield to deflect and delegitimize the criticisms from Brussels. . . . As experts in European politics and the religious right, we argue that Orbán's embrace of religion has served to consolidate his power, "other" his opponents and shield Hungary from EU criticism of its attacks on the rule of law. . . . It is also, we believe, a dangerous model for how religion can be used to fuel democratic backsliding.[16]

Gallaher and Martin tell the tale of Orbán's evolution from an atheistic politician to a self-styled defender of Christian Hungary and Christian Europe. In the 1990s, he renounced his atheism, and he is today a member of the Hungarian Reformed Church. After

---

15. "Conservative Political Action Conference, Hungarian Prime Minister Viktor Orbán Remarks," C-Span, August 4, 2022, https://tinyurl.com/yckysh2m; Justin Spike, "Hungarian Nationalist PM to Deliver Speech at CPAC," Associated Press, July 11, 2022, https://tinyurl.com/38unurks; "Speech by Prime Minister Viktor Orbán at the 31st Bálványos Summer Free University and Student Camp," July 23, 2022, Prime Minister, https://tinyurl.com/dd8bdy9j.

16. Gallaher and Martin, "Orbán's Use and Misuse of Religion."

he was voted out in 2002, Orbán "vowed not to lose power again if he ever returned to office." He has spent the last twelve years ruthlessly consolidating his power. One way he has found to do that is by exploiting Hungarian religiosity. Though Hungary is both more religiously diverse and secular than either Poland or Russia, he has gained success with this strategy.

Orbán began styling himself as an advocate of "Christian democracy" right after 2010. But in doing so since then he has leaned heavily on the negative possibilities that this could offer him, rather than by casting any positive vision. He has turned his aim on what, and whom, Christians should be against: Muslim refugees, European liberals, gay people, trans people, feminists, "wokeness," and George Soros, the wealthy Hungarian Jewish Holocaust survivor whose foundation actually funded part of Orbán's education.

On this last obsession, the antisemitic tropes deployed in this bit of 2018 propaganda about Soros will be familiar to anyone who has studied that toxic tradition: "We are fighting an enemy that is different from us. Not open, but hiding; not straightforward, but crafty; not honest, but base; not national, but international; does not believe in working, but speculates with money."[17] This is classic antisemitism. It is immensely dangerous when government officials speak this way about Jews, or for that matter when they use their immense platforms to target any person or group.

Christians who believe in and value democracy should resist leaders who weaken it, even if those leaders say some words that affirm Christianity and criticize those who make Christians uneasy. But in Hungary, Viktor Orbán has once again found that Christians are easily swayed by religious rhetoric and by policies that seem to roll back cultural developments that they find unwelcome. He has remade Hungary as an illiberal Christian autocracy. Perhaps that is precisely what many Christians in Hungary want. It is a textbook example of authoritarian reactionary Christianity.

17. Gallaher and Martin, "Orbán's Use and Misuse of Religion."

The ingenious creativity both of Orbán's political use of Christianity and of his subversion of liberal democracy for illiberal autocracy has not been lost on his fellow travelers in other countries, including Brazil and the United States. Donald Trump has warmly endorsed him as a kindred spirit, and Trump advisor Steve Bannon called Orbán "Trump before Trump."[18] It is to Brazil and the United States we now turn.

18. Marantz, "Illiberal Order," 46.

10

Authoritarian Reactionary Christianity in Bolsonaro's Brazil

> Bolsonaro has established himself as a right-wing, pan-Christian figure who unites conservative competitors in the religious marketplace—Catholics and evangelicals—around a mythical representation of Brazil's past and an imagined project for its future.
>
> —Raimundo Barreto and João Chaves
>
> (2021)[1]

Brazil has attracted considerable international attention due to the high visibility of its president from 2018 to 2022, Jair Bolsonaro. Bolsonaro is a Catholic-evangelical hybrid politician with a base of conservative religious support strongly resembling that of former US president Donald Trump. Indeed, the politics of the two movements are so closely connected as to be fairly considered one movement, and there has been plenty of engagement back and forth between right-wing political and religious figures in the two countries. Historian Benjamin Cowan argues that "Brazil and the United States have constructed together a transnational religious right."[2] This transnational religious right happens to demonstrate consis-

---

1. Raimundo Barreto and João Chaves, "Christian Nationalism Is Thriving in Bolsonaro's Brazil," *Christian Century*, December 1, 2021, 23.
2. Quoted in Barreto and Chaves, "Christian Nationalism," 23.

tent antidemocratic and authoritarian tendencies. We have been examining this movement far beyond Brazil and the United States, but the similarities only seem to deepen as we move to the Americas.

Brazil's Weakening Democratic Health under Bolsonaro

Freedom House offered the following summary of the democratic health of Brazil as of early 2022:

> Brazil is a democracy that holds competitive elections, and the political arena, though polarized, is characterized by vibrant public debate. However, independent journalists and civil society activists risk harassment and violent attack, and the government has struggled to address high rates of violent crime and disproportionate violence against and economic exclusion of minorities. Corruption is endemic at top levels, contributing to widespread disillusionment with traditional political parties. Societal discrimination and violence against LGBT+ people remain serious problems.[3]

Bolsonaro, a former army captain, began his term as president in 2018. He ran as the representative of the misnamed far-right Social-Liberal Party, winning with 55 percent of the vote. Freedom House starkly describes his campaign as "characterized by a disdain for democratic principles." The *Economist* describes Bolsonaro as "an avowed authoritarian who is contemptuous of the judiciary and the separation of powers."[4] The campaign atmosphere in 2018 was polarized, tense, and violent, with most threats and attacks on media members, candidates, supporters, and members of the judiciary carried out by Bolsonaro supporters. Bolsonaro himself was stabbed during his first presidential campaign, which took him off the campaign trail for a month and gained him some sympathy votes.

---

3. "Freedom in the World 2022: Brazil," Freedom House, https://tinyurl.com/5yh35aan.
4. "The Battle for Brazil," *Economist*, April 2, 2022, 26.

Anti-LGBTQ+, Anti-Science, Claims of Election Fraud: Sound Familiar?

Bolsonaro's agenda was established in his inaugural address: "Let's unite the people, value the family, respect religions and our Judeo-Christian tradition, fight gender ideology, and preserve our values. Brazil will once again be a country free from ideological shackles."[5] This framing obviously shares features with the reactionary religio-moral, antiliberal, anti-inclusive agenda we noted in relation to Russia, Poland, and Hungary, again strongly supported by conservative Christians. "Ideological shackles" here means any current of thought that fully includes historically marginalized groups along axes of race, gender, sexuality, and religious conviction.

Seeing the consistent pattern of demagoguery in relation to LGBTQ+ people in all the countries we have studied so far, I pause here to note how wrong it is that targeting this group is so often the means by which conservative Christian populists gain power. It is a strategy of evoking disgust for a group of vulnerable people and then leveraging that disgust to gain political power. This is abusive and can be deadly—and it is especially egregious when done in the name of Jesus, who taught love of neighbor.

Barreto and Chaves describe "the cultlike movement that animates Bolsonaro's base" as against "moral relativism, social liberalism, alleged neo-Marxism in its various forms, and LGBTQ rights," and as "pro-gun . . . anti-Black, [and] anti-democracy." In practice, Bolsonaro's reign has also weakened the social safety net, ramping up hunger and poverty, and increasing corruption.

Bolsonaro, like US president Donald Trump, was also hugely negligent in relation to COVID. Bolsonaro described COVID as "a little flu," refused vaccination, and delayed in buying vaccines for Brazil when they first were developed. All of this was with the strong support of conservative Christians and their leaders, who were susceptible to anti-scientific quackery and who promoted it on their platforms. Bra-

5. Barreto and Chaves, "Christian Nationalism," 23.

zilian scientists project that at least a third of Brazil's 660,000 COVID deaths were preventable,[6] and that primary responsibility for Brazil's vast death rate rests with Bolsonaro and his backers.

Human Rights Watch joined other worried observers as far back as 2020 in expressing concern that Bolsonaro was a threat to democracy in Brazil: "He is pursuing campaigns to intimidate the Supreme Court, signaling that he may attempt to cancel the 2022 election or otherwise deny Brazilians the right to elect their leaders, and violating critics' freedom of expression."[7] Fortunately, despite his machinations, Bolsonaro was able neither to cancel nor to nullify the October 2022 election, which he lost by a few percentage points to his rival Luiz Inácio Lula da Silva. But it appears that his inability to follow through on his threats was due to the quick and unchallenged vote count and the immediate unified response of the leadership of Brazil's House, Senate, Supreme Court, and attorney general, as well as the military's disinterest in intervening. Bolsonaro never did concede his election loss, but he was boxed in and lacked the ability to do anything about it.

This was a far better outcome than what might have been expected. Bolsonaro began claiming in 2021 that the upcoming election might be rigged using electronic voting machines to defraud him. He threatened in April 2022 that the elections could be "suspended" if "something abnormal happens."[8] He also suggested that he could not lose a fair election and threatened not to honor the result of any election that went against him. "Only God can get me out of this seat," Bolsonaro repeatedly said.[9] As the *Economist* commented in July 2022: "He tells supporters he can only lose if the election is rigged. This suggests he may dispute the result if he loses. What is unclear is how far he might go, and who might support him

6. Barreto and Chaves, "Christian Nationalism," 24.

7. "Brazil: Bolsonaro Threatens Democratic Rule," Human Rights Watch, September 15, 2021, https://tinyurl.com/54cuptjk.

8. Ciara Nugent, "Lula the Redeemer," *Time*, May 23/30, 2022, 68.

9. Barreto and Chaves, "Christian Nationalism," 24.

if he plays dirty.["10] This script sounds familiar to anyone who has endured the last several years in the United States.

Bolsonaro tilted heavily in the direction of the military, a worrying sign of authoritarianism. Not only did he express support for Brazil's military dictatorship of 1964–1985; he said in 2016 that the main mistake of the military dictatorship was that it had merely tortured rather than killed enemies of the state.[11] Bolsonaro's administration was also filled with retired and active-duty military figures, and he deployed the military in some worrisome ways for non-military tasks. We are reminded that a key aspect of healthy democracy is an apolitical military with strict commitments to democracy. That military came through for Brazil by keeping those commitments in October 2022.

The area of media freedom is another area of grave concern in Brazil. As in several other of the countries we have studied, journalists in Bolsonaro's Brazil routinely were harassed, threatened, sued, and targeted for violence. Laws protecting the press are too weak, according to Freedom House, leaving even opinion columnists at risks of being sued, for example, for negative coverage of the government's handling of COVID.

Brazil's constitution promises equal rights to all, but discrimination against Afro-Brazilians, Indigenous Brazilians, and LGBTQ+ people appears to have accelerated during the Bolsonaro years. In 2018, a Black lesbian Rio de Janeiro politician, Marielle Franco, was murdered. Investigations "revealed business-government corruption schemes and the growing power of militia groups in Rio de Janeiro State, whose membership includes active and retired members of the local police force." Violent homophobic rhetoric is, in general, creating a threatening environment for that community. Brazil is reported to have one of the world's highest rates of violence

---

10. "Might Bolsonaro Try to Steal the Vote?" *Economist*, July 16, 2022, 32.

11. "Defender of the Dictatorship, Jair Bolsonaro Reinforces Controversial Phrase, 'The Mistake Was to Torture and Not to Kill,'" Jovem Pan News, July 8, 2016, https://tinyurl.com/39jac8fe.

against LGBTQ+ people. Transgender people are especially targeted for violence.

As in Hungary, academic freedom was threatened and impinged upon in Bolsonaro's Brazil, especially when the government wished to suppress criticism. Sensitive issues included COVID, biodiversity, land rights, and climate change. As is increasingly visible in the United States as well, race and gender issues have become sensitive at the K–12 level. Freedom House says that the Bolsonaro administration "sought to remove references to gender-based violence (GBV) and minority-rights issues from school textbooks." Some educators, administrators, and researchers have been leaving the profession or even leaving the country.

Brazil is listed as a "free" country by Freedom House, with an overall score of 73/100. At the time of writing, its democracy remains intact. Its political situation seems remarkably like that of the United States, in this sense: Brazil elected a conservative populist demonstrating antidemocratic impulses, with the strong support of Catholic and fundamentalist/evangelical voters who liked his positions on religion and culture-wars issues.

Another Favorite of a Catholic-Evangelical Coalition

Barreto and Chaves lay responsibility for the rise of Jair Bolsonaro in Brazil very much at the feet of a powerful Catholic-evangelical coalition. Catholicism was, of course, the dominant religion in Brazil from colonial days. Its power waned, however, as fundamentalism, Evangelicalism, and Pentecostalism swept the country, beginning in the first half of the twentieth century. Charismatic Catholicism is a kind of Catholic-Pentecostal hybrid. Bolsonaro himself is right at this intersection, a Catholic with an evangelical wife who got himself quite visibly rebaptized as an adult in the Jordan River in 2018. Bolsonaro's skillful combining of Protestant and Catholic identity helped him glue together a conservative religious coalition that can unite around shared enemies.

The hunger of Brazil's growing evangelical population for political power, which has such strong parallels in the United States, needs to be given a moment of attention. As of May 2022, 195 of Brazil's lower house's 513 national deputies belonged to the evangelical caucus.[12] That's 38 percent. Bolsonaro governed as the first evangelical president. Getting an evangelical elected president had long been a cherished goal for that community. Unfortunately, evangelical voters seem mainly to seek leaders who will advance their institutional interests and defeat social inclusion for marginalized groups. As far back as 2007, a scholarly study of evangelical politics in Latin America drew the following conclusions:

> Evangelicals who play the game of politics prove no less subject than others to its characteristic dynamics and temptations, including the corporatist pursuit of narrow group interests over against the common good and participation in corrupt patron-client relations. . . . Evangelicals who seek to enhance their political recognition and influence by any means whatsoever soon see their integrity, reputation, *and* political influence suffer one setback after another.[13]

As we prepare to study the United States, it is relevant to note the connections between the religious cultures of the two countries, which helps make sense of the similarities in the politics of the two countries. During the twentieth century, Brazil was the target of constant missionary efforts, especially from Southern Baptists. Even today the influence of conservative American Christianity on Brazilian theology and church life is very evident. The similarity is also evident when it comes to the way in which politics seems to

---

12. "The Cross on the Ballot," *Economist*, May 14, 2022, 29.

13. Timothy Samuel Shah, preface to *Evangelical Christianity and Democracy in Latin America*, ed. Paul Freston (Oxford: Oxford University Press, 2008), xiii.

trump personal morality. In Brazil, massive numbers of Christians supported a "traditional-values" politician who has been married three times and fathered five children, one with a mistress.[14] The similarity to the Trump marital history is rather striking.

In terms of the personal Trump/Bolsonaro connection, Barreto and Chaves report this news:

> Bolsonaro and his influential sons are strongly pro-American, having close ties to Donald Trump and his former advisor Steve Bannon, among others. Bolsonaro's son, the senator Eduardo Bolsonaro, often joins Bannon in his far-right nationalist, but ironically transnational, crusades. On January 4, [2021], Eduardo arrived "by surprise" at the White House. On January 5 he spent the day meeting with the Trump family and supporters, and the next day [the fateful January 6] he was photographed in DC wearing a Trump 2020 election hat.[15]

Democracy in the Balance (Again)

As with the United States in 2020, when Brazilians voted in October 2022, a vote for Bolsonaro was a vote for autocracy. He just barely lost, and he still retains the strong support of conservative Christians, attracted to Bolsonaro's version of authoritarian reactionary Christianity and happy to receive their share of the spoils of power. The Bolsonaro movement is not dead, and authoritarian reactionary Christians remain at its center. The threat to democracy in Brazil may not yet be over.

14. I am grateful to Andre Lisboa for this observation, via private communication with the author.

15. Barreto and Chaves, "Christian Nationalism," 23.

11

Authoritarian Reactionary Christianity in Trump's United States

America is the last bastion of Christian freedom. It's the last bastion of capitalism. . . . I declare unto you that President Donald Trump is gonna stay for four more years in the White House. . . . We're a mighty army. They've gotta listen. They can't ignore us. Our churches have been backed into a corner. . . . We pray for Enrique [Tarrio], and Lord, we pray for his organization [the Proud Boys]. And Lord, they may get a bum rap on the news media, but we just thank God that we can lock shields, and we can come shoulder-to-shoulder with people that still stand up for this nation, and still love the rights and the freedoms that we have 'cause Lord, we've gotta recognize the fact if we don't have convictions worth dying for, we don't even know what living really is. So, God, help us to live, help us to fight, and if need be, lay down our life for this nation.

—US pastor Greg Locke
(January 5, 2021)[1]

---

1. Quoted in the astonishing report by Andrew Seidel, "Events, People, and Networks Leading Up to January 6," in "Christian Nationalism and the January 6 Insurrection," Baptist Joint Committee, February 9, 2022,

CHAPTER 11

I am a lifetime citizen of the United States and have followed news
and politics closely here for fifty years. That makes this chapter
harder rather than easier to write. I know too much and care too
deeply. I have seen better days and have been anguished by recent
developments. I write with the broken heart of a frightened US patriot and mortified US Christian. To steady my approach and ensure
as much objectivity as possible, I will attempt to follow the same
paradigm as in the other country chapters, beginning with external
commentary based on the standard democracy criteria.

Freedom House, reporting in early 2022, gives the US an overall
democracy score of 83/100 in its country report—32/40 in political
rights, 51/60 in civil liberties. Freedom House summarizes the
health of US democracy as follows:

> The United States is a federal republic whose people benefit
> from a vibrant political system, a strong rule-of-law tradition,
> robust freedoms of expression and religious belief, and a wide
> array of other civil liberties. However, in recent years its dem-
> ocratic institutions have suffered erosion, as reflected in rising
> political polarization and extremism, partisan pressure on the
> electoral process, bias and dysfunction in the criminal justice
> system, harmful policies on immigration and asylum seekers,
> and growing disparities in wealth, economic opportunity, and
> political influence.[2]

January 6, 2021: A Jolt to the Peaceful Transfer of Power

Freedom House describes the events after the November 2020
presidential election in this way: "The transfer of power from the
administration of President Donald Trump to that of President Jo-

---

https://tinyurl.com/3zv36j92. Every American, at least, should study
this document.

2. "Freedom in the World: United States," Freedom House, https://
tinyurl.com/ypa7ws49.

seph Biden in January was seriously threatened by a series of anti-democratic actions intended to thwart it." That measured remark seems the right way to describe it based on what we know as of August 2022. The peaceful transfer of power, one of the hallmarks of democracy, was indeed "seriously threatened." It was threatened by "a series of antidemocratic actions," not just what happened on January 6, which was only the culmination of that series of actions. Representative Liz Cheney, the brave conservative Republican from Wyoming who serves as vice chair of the January 6 committee of the United States Congress, and who has been voted out of office by her Republican constituency for her efforts to tell the truth about Trump's threats to the peaceful transfer of power, outlined the seven steps of this effort:

1. President Trump engaged in a massive effort to spread false and fraudulent information to the American public, claiming the 2020 election was stolen from him.
2. President Trump corruptly planned to replace the acting attorney general, so that the Department of Justice would support his fake election claims.
3. President Trump corruptly pressured Vice President Pence to refuse to count certified electoral votes in violation of the US Constitution and the law.
4. President Trump corruptly pressured state election officials, and state legislators, to change election results.
5. President Trump's legal team and other Trump associates instructed Republicans in multiple states to create false electoral slates and transmit those slates to Congress and the National Archives.
6. President Trump summoned and assembled a violent mob in Washington and directed them to march on the US Capitol. [Note: Evidence has been presented that he also planned to march with them to the Capitol but was prevented from doing so by his security detail.]
7. As the violence was underway, President Trump ignored multi-

ple pleas for assistance and failed to take immediate action to stop the violence and instruct his supporters to leave the Capitol.[3]

At the time of this writing, the January 6 committee has presented its compelling evidence for each of these seven steps in a series of public hearings. Hundreds of arrests and multiple convictions of those who breached the Capitol have been made. It seems apparent that the United States Justice Department and prosecutors in other relevant venues are considering prosecution of Donald Trump and his associates who were involved in this deadly plot, which culminated in the worst attack on the US Capitol since the War of 1812.

The Day a President Threatened Democracy Itself

The fundamental issue with Donald Trump and those who supported him, some all the way to the attack on the Capitol, is not that he embraced predictable right-wing policy preferences strongly supported by culturally conservative Christians. If such policies are the will of enough people, they are likely to prevail through more-or-less normal democratic processes. That has happened, for example, with the Supreme Court of the United States overturning a federally guaranteed right to abortion in the summer of 2022, a decision which, whatever else one might say about it, may have helped conservative, anti-abortion Christians regain a bit of confidence in the American political process.[4]

3. Dana Bash, Jake Tapper, and Jeremy Herb, "January 6 Vice Chair Cheney Said Trump Had a 'Seven-Part Plan' to Overturn the Election. Here's What She Meant," CNN, June 10, 2022, https://tinyurl.com/3ejteceb.
4. Consider these words from conservative Catholic researcher/writer Mary Eberstadt: "In the battles between those who believe the United States to be irredeemable without *radical new arrangements* and those who do not, a gale wind of momentum has just been sent the latter's way. . . . The federalism that remains one of the wonders of the political world came through. It came through in a way that many . . . had despaired of ever hap-

What happened in late 2020 and early 2021 was that, for the first time in US history, a president threatened democracy itself. That should matter—it must matter—more than any Christian's policy preference on any issue. It seems a bit late for a country with a 240-year-old democracy to begin a process of "democratic deconsolidation,"[5] but that is what we witnessed during the Trump administration. January 6 was the culmination of authoritarian tendencies visible from the moment the Trump campaign was launched. It also marked a terrible advance in the radicalization of a significant number of authoritarian reactionary American Christians.

As Steven Levitzky and Daniel Ziblatt already argued in a book published in 2018, completed not long after Trump took office, Trump's authoritarian tendencies were visible from the time of his first campaign in summer 2015. Anyone who studies political authoritarianism could see the warning signs, which we outlined earlier: his rejection of democratic rules of the game, denial of the legitimacy of political opponents, toleration or encouragement of political violence, and readiness to curtail the civil liberties of opponents, including the media.[6]

---

pening again." Mary Eberstadt, "What the Nurses Knew," *National Review*, August 1, 2022, 21, italics added. Conservative columnist Ross Douthat of the *New York Times* made a similar point before the *Roe v. Wade* decision was overturned: "From the religious perspective, meanwhile, by constitutionalizing the issue Roe didn't just deliver a normal political defeat; it seemed to read certain convictions out of the American constitutional order entirely, seeding a religious alienation that continues to bear bitter fruit today." Ross Douthat, "How Roe Warped the Republic," *New York Times*, May 8, 2022, C9. Now that access to abortion has largely been taken away from one-third of American women, a political backlash is growing. Democracy is not done with the abortion issue, it seems.

5. Roberto Stefan Foa and Yascha Mounk, "The Signs of Deconsolidation," *Journal of Democracy* 28, no. 1 (January 2017): 5-16, https://tinyurl.com/meatpzy.

6. Steven Levitsky and Daniel Ziblatt, *How Democracies Die* (New York: Broadway Books, 2018), 23-24.

Democratic Erosion in a Once-Consolidated Democracy

Today we see the bitter fruits of a new kind of threat to democracy having taken root in the United States. In early 2022, Freedom House summarized the main aspects of democratic erosion under Trump, and under his influence. I report a few of the most salient, and add notes about developments since their report:

- Creating a massive disinformation campaign about election processes and results, undercutting trust in election processes, creating a threatening environment for election workers, attempting to intimidate or entice state-level officials to change vote results, encouraging public demonstrations against the election, and delegitimizing the newly elected president. Current: Most Republican candidates standing for election in Fall 2022 won their primaries by repeating some version of Donald Trump's election-rigging claims.
- Encouraging creation of an environment for state-level officials to undercut fairness in election administration moving forward, in part by campaigning against officials who refused to cooperate with his election-subversion efforts and by elevating new candidates whose abject fealty to him and his disinformation threatens the fairness of future election administration. Current: Many Republicans who publicly refused to accept Trump's election disinformation were targeted by him for defeat in their primaries, and many did lose. Election-deniers are running for many of the very offices that manage local and state elections.
- Creating the conditions for, as Freedom House says, "a broader rise in violence and intimidation as a tool of political influence in the United States. Numerous known affiliates of right-wing extremist groups participated in the attack [on January 6], and many Republicans and far-right media figures later sought to recast it as a patriotic protest or a defense of election integrity. The documented participation of military veterans in the vio-

lence prompted the Defense Department to order a broad review of measures necessary to minimize extremist behavior among active-duty troops." Current: Threats of political violence remain high.

· Refusing to cooperate with most congressional oversight functions, including mandated reports, oversight, and subpoenas for testimony. The Trump administration's refusal to cooperate with the presidential transition was unprecedented and hindered the launch of the new Biden administration. Current: Many Trump-related officials have refused to submit to or have gone to court to fight congressional and state-level subpoenas.

· Flouting government ethics rules and norms, especially in the area of financial conflicts of interest. One example was the directing of government events to Trump properties. Current: Donald Trump's transport, retention, hiding, and then refusal to return highly classified government documents violated not just government ethics rules but federal law.

· Ignoring requirements for information transparency, actively promoting disinformation, including on COVID, and weakening executive branch auditing and investigative offices.

· Creating a hostile and sometimes threatening environment for journalists, who also became targets of arrest and violence as they covered major news stories such as the protests related to the death of George Floyd at the hands of Minnesota police officers.

· Regularly encouraging violence against protestors at his political rallies in 2016. Later, Trump encouraged harsh police crackdowns on Black Lives Matter protests. He threatened to deploy the military in cities facing unrest. It may be that only strong traditions of military non-involvement in domestic politics prevented major lines from being crossed here.

· Abusing the presidential pardon power, often to set free his political cronies. Trump has publicly attempted to intimidate and tamper with witnesses in various investigations related to him. He has attempted to influence the decisions of judges, including the Supreme Court, ruling on election-related matters. Fortunately, the tradition of judicial independence largely held. Current: Trump's allies were discussing and seeking preemptive pardons from him for their efforts to help him overturn the election. The Justice Department is attempting to protect the identity of FBI agents and witnesses in the classified documents investigation because of likely or actual threats against them.

This final point is my own:

- Contributing to an environment of hostility and violence reported by Hispanic, Middle Eastern, African, and Asian Americans and visitors triggered by Trump's harsh rhetoric and policies. Added to his comments in relation to the Black Lives Matter movement and attacks on Black athletes protesting police brutality, the Trump years created the environment for a surge of white ethno-nationalism and extremism in the United States.

See No Evil: Trump's Loyal Christian Enablers

None of this appeared to shake in any serious way the support of conservative Christian people in the United States for the person who continues to pose the single greatest threat to American democracy since the Civil War of the mid-nineteenth century. Indeed, it has reshaped the evangelical community in his image.[7] Trump famously marveled during his first campaign that he could stand in the streets and shoot someone, and his supporters would still follow him.[8] He was just beginning to wrap his mind around that discovery.

7. Gregory A. Smith, "More White Americans Adopted Than Shed Evangelical Label during Trump Presidency, Especially His Supporters," Pew Research Center, September 15, 2021, https://tinyurl.com/4u4pv99a/.

8. Jeremy Diamond, "Trump: I Could 'Shoot Somebody and I Wouldn't Lose Voters,'" CNN, January 24, 2016, https://tinyurl.com/tt9jzn8j.

It remains the single most important fact today. He did stand outside the White House and send down to the Capitol thousands of enraged believers in his lie of a stolen election, with deadly results, and yet many of his supporters still follow him. Some of these hard-core Trumpists have proven that they would willingly support the unprecedented overturning of the results of a democratic election if their hero said that the election was invalid.

Robert Jones's Public Religion Research Institute found in their August 2021 polling that 34 percent of all Americans polled completely or mostly agree that Donald Trump is a "true patriot," while 29 percent completely or mostly agree that the 2020 election was "stolen" from him. Among white evangelical Protestants, those respective numbers were 68 percent and 61 percent. [9]

Trump gained this loyalty using many of the same strategies we have outlined in our previous country studies. With the notable exception of gay-bashing, Trump used the authoritarian reactionary Christian playbook. He would bring conservative Christians access to power, and he would use his own power to advance many of their goals. He delivered on what he promised, more than any prior president in the nearly fifty years of the Republican Party strategy of partnering with the Christian Right to win elections.

Ever-Deeper Right-Wing Radicalization

It seems clear that some of Trump's Christian followers have bypassed him in their radicalization. When politicians like the Republican congresswoman Lauren Boebert (R-CO) question the separation of US church and state, they are not *ignorant*, as some critics suggest. They are *radical*, in relation to challenging our 240-year-old constitutional disestablishment of state religion. [10] When pastors publicly

9. Statistics provided to me by Robert Jones, via private communication with the author.

10. Adela Suliman and Timothy Bella, "GOP Rep. Boebert: 'I'm Tired of

applaud right-wing militias like the Proud Boys, on the eve of the attack on the Capitol, they are not just participating in Christian nationalism. They are inflaming right-wing religious/insurrectionist violence. We have witnessed in our time the movement of some beyond Christian "culture wars" to actual Christian holy violence.

Some of the Republican candidates running for office in Fall 2022 were an entirely new and frightening breed. Pennsylvania gubernatorial candidate Doug Mastriano was a notable example.[11] A visibly devout fundamentalist Christian, he helped lead the 2020 "Stop the Steal" movement in Pennsylvania. He then chartered buses to take like-minded Pennsylvanians to Washington on January 6. He passed by police barricades that day, though he claims he never entered the Capitol. His actions remain under investigation. Fortunately, like a number of other radicalized Trumpist candidates, he was defeated in the November 2022 elections.

A Brief Excursus on "Democracy" versus "Republic"

During his doomed campaign, Doug Mastriano mocked the idea that the United States is a "democracy," instead saying that we are a "republic." He was not the first to do so in recent years. This arcane theoretical distinction has been retrieved on the far right, from the deep-fringe territory of the radical John Birch Society,[12] apparently

---

This Separation of Church and State Junk,'" MSN, June 28, 2022, https://tinyurl.com/bdzf9fk4.

11. The details that follow are reported by Charles Homans, "'Stop the Steal' Forever," *New York Times Magazine*, July 24, 2022, 22–31, 46–49. Similar reporting focusing on the equally radical candidates in Arizona is offered in Robert Draper, "The Arizona Experiment," *New York Times Magazine*, August 21, 2022, 42–47.

12. The John Birch Society, which still exists, is an extreme far-right group that became famous in the 1960s for its ferocious anti-Communism and conspiracy thinking. See John Savage, "The John Birch Society Is Back," *Politico Magazine*, July 16, 2017, https://tinyurl.com/mr3d7jbz.

to suggest that states/legislators rather than the voters should determine presidential electoral votes or that conservative Christian values rather than majority vote preferences should prevail. This is such an important example of an effort to destabilize the current practice of US democracy that it is worth lingering over for a moment.

There is no consensus on the precise meaning of the word "republican," partly because it has evolved over many centuries. Its origin is the Latin *res publica*, simply meaning "public thing" or "public matter." A core meaning of a republican understanding of government is that the political community is a public matter rather than the private possession of a monarch or ruling family. Republicanism is anti-royalist and anti-dictatorial; this at least appears to be agreed.

The term can be traced to the Roman Republic (509-27 BCE), which was essentially a form of aristocratic rule through the Roman Senate. It could not be described as a democracy, as in the ancient Athenian democracy, though the Roman Republic had certain modestly democratic elements. The Roman Republic ended when rule was seized by Caesar in 27 BCE and Rome became an imperial dictatorship.

Today, scores of the world's countries declare themselves to be "republics," and their governance varies dramatically. In common usage, "republic" tends to mean "representative democracy," in the sense of a mixed system employing representative rather than direct democracy and intentionally checking majoritarian power in a variety of ways.

We note that the US Constitution (Article IV.4) "guarantees to every State in this Union a republican form of government," and the term "democracy" is not used. The *Federalist Papers*, a brilliant extended commentary on the proposed US Constitution written by James Madison, Alexander Hamilton, and John Jay, differentiates a democracy from a republic in this way: in a republic, the people delegate power to representatives that they elect, rather than attempting direct democracy in which all gather to debate and decide. *Federalist* 10 argues that this approach has the advantages of entrusting leadership to especially wise and discerning citizens and of enabling the governance of a larger number of people and greater extent of territory than would be possible in a direct democracy.[13] In modern business parlance, a republic can be scaled up. But this is simply a distinction in the *strategy* for arranging the people's self-rule, rather than a rejection of democracy. At the time of the birth of the United States, it was common parlance to say that "democrats" opposed monarchy and sought to create a "republican" system instead. That still makes sense. The distinction between "democracy" and "republic" cannot legitimately be pressed in the way right-wing antidemocratic voices are attempting.

"General Opposition to the Constitutional Order"

Donald Trump was defeated in 2020, and he (barely) vacated the White House in January 2021. With this near miss, and the inauguration of Joe Biden as president, the United States bought a few more years to decide whether our democracy will survive. Much depends on what that massive number of white American Christians decide to do if, despite everything, Donald Trump is again a serious candidate for president in 2024.

Unfortunately, it may not even be about Trump anymore. Sober-minded conservative observers like Matthew Continetti, in his massive recent book on the last hundred years of American conservativism, are acknowledging the current radicalization of the Republican electorate: "Many on the right embraced a cult of personality and illiberal tropes. The danger was that the alienation

13. *The Federalist Papers*, no. 10 (New York: Signet Classic Edition, 1999), 76–79. In *Federalist* 14, Madison writes: "In a democracy the people meet and exercise the government in person; in a republic, they assemble and administer it by their representatives. . . . A democracy, consequently, must be confined to a small spot. A republic may be extended over a large region" (95).

from and antagonism toward American culture and society expressed by many on the right could turn into a general opposition to the constitutional order."[14]

Seeing no repentance from radicalized authoritarian reactionaries, many of them Christians, I find it hard to be terribly hopeful of a change of heart. Criminal justice officials will pursue their investigations, and Donald Trump and his closest associates may be forced from public life. But the deeper sources of the fever that has gripped our politics will remain.

14. Matthew Continetti, *The Right: The Hundred Year War for American Conservatism* (New York: Basic Books, 2022), 411.

12

The Baptist Democratic Tradition

The Baptists had . . . insisted that the way Jesus made
disciples was by teaching and persuasion, not by coercion. They held that the government has no com-
petence in religion, and when it seeks to enforce faith
it creates wars of religion and hypocrites who claim
a faith they do not actually hold. . . . [F]ollowing a
thicker Jesus rules out coercion and thus contributes
to religious liberty. The sovereignty of God through
all of life requires Christian responsibility in every
area and thus bestows democracy to society.

—Glen Harold Stassen (2012)[1]

We have now been immersed in some disastrous versions of
Christian politics. I have argued that all can be described
as expressions of authoritarian reactionary Christianity, usually
based on cultural nostalgia for a lost world *back there*. These Christians are filled with yearnings for an organically Christian national
life; angry about social changes interpreted as godless, immoral,
and oppressive; and willing to consider antidemocratic politics by
way of response.

---

1. Glen Harold Stassen, *A Thicker Jesus: Incarnational Discipleship for a
Secular Age* (Louisville: Westminster John Knox, 2012), 66.

Alexis de Tocqueville, that great early nineteenth-century observer of the early democracies of France and the United States, saw the problem clearly:

> Christianity, which has declared that all men are equal in the sight of God, will not refuse to acknowledge that all citizens are equal in the eyes of the law. But, by a singular concourse of events, religion has been for a time entangled with those institutions which democracy assails; and it is not unfrequently brought to reject the equality which it loves, and to curse that cause of liberty as a foe, whose efforts it might hallow by its alliance.[2]

Authoritarian reactionary Christianity turns out to be a global phenomenon, affecting historically Roman Catholic, Eastern Orthodox, and Protestant lands. Its antiliberalism has very deep roots, and that antiliberalism has intensified in successive waves over the last fifty years. It is in the marrow of hundreds of millions of Christians, and it has been wired into right-wing politics in many countries, such that leveraging its passion can help ambitious politicians gain power. It will not go away easily. It is easier to describe a problem than to propose solutions. I cannot really say that what I will offer in the next three chapters constitutes a solution. However, I will attempt to sketch certain historic resources that may help create a better Christian posture toward the world we live in and a renewed Christian commitment to democracy. These three resources are the Baptist democratic tradition, the Black Christian democratic tradition, and the democratic covenantal tradition. We will take each in turn over the final three chapters.

2. Alexis de Tocqueville, *Democracy in America* (New York: New American Library, 1956), 34.

An Ode to My Democracy-Loving Mentor

We begin with what I will describe as the Baptist democratic tradition, though it could also be called the free church, believers' church, congregationalist church, or dissenting church democratic tradition. Our primary guide will be my own teacher, Glen Harold Stassen (1936–2014). And here I must say a personal word.

Every scholar is trained within a particular tradition and by crucial mentors. My primary mentor was Glen Stassen. Stassen was a Baptist ethicist trained at Southern Baptist Theological Seminary, Union Theological Seminary in New York, and Duke University, with post-doctoral work at Harvard University. He initiated me into the field of Christian ethics at Southern Seminary. Stassen encouraged my PhD admission to Union, where I was supervised by Larry Rasmussen, then holder of the Reinhold Niebuhr Chair. Stassen, Rasmussen, and I all shared deep interests in the German Church Struggle, the Holocaust, and nuclear-era peacemaking.

Finishing at Union with a dissertation on Christians who rescued Jews during the Holocaust,[3] I returned to Southern Seminary as a junior professor. There, from 1993 to 1996, Stassen and I endured that school's turn to the authoritarian reactionary Christian right, before we both took other posts. We eventually wrote a Christian ethics textbook together—*Kingdom Ethics*[4]—and our work remains very closely identified.

The towering influence of Glen's father, Harold Stassen, must be understood if one wants to understand the ethics of the son.[5] Harold Stassen was a leading liberal Republican—a political tribe

3. Published as David P. Gushee, *The Righteous Gentiles of the Holocaust: A Christian Interpretation* (Minneapolis: Fortress, 1994).

4. Having sold well over 30,000 copies and been translated into multiple languages, the book remains in print in a second edition. David P. Gushee and Glen H. Stassen, *Kingdom Ethics: Following Jesus in Contemporary Context*, 2nd ed. (Grand Rapids: Eerdmans, 2016).

5. The authoritative biography is Alec Kirby, David G. Dalin, and

now extinct. Minnesota elected him, at thirty-one, as the youngest governor in US history. Governor Stassen resigned his office to serve in the navy during World War II. He helped to draft the charter of the United Nations. In 1948, he very nearly became the Republican nominee for president, and had a very good chance of winning if nominated. He eventually served in the cabinet of President Dwight Eisenhower, first managing foreign aid and then nuclear arms negotiations.

Perhaps this helps to explain some of the reasons why his son Glen Stassen so "loved democracy,"[6] as another of his graduates, Ron Sanders, has put it. Glen was a firmly democratic Baptist ethicist. In this he reflected the legacy of his illustrious family.

But Glen's support for democracy was not just based on his family background. It was developed in his scholarship, in his just peacemaking theory, in his account of the historical development of democracy, and in his advocacy for a Christian democratic vision and practice. It is Stassen's broad scholarly engagement with democracy that I want to engage here.

Making the Christian Case for Democracy

Glen Stassen was probably best known for his seminal just peacemaking theory, which aimed to propose verifiably effective global practices for making just peace, and to help Christians get beyond the older debate about whether war is ever morally permissible.

Stassen argued that democracy contributes to global justice and peace. He included "advancing democracy, justice, and human rights" as one of the core practices of this peacemaking theory. In

---

John F. Rothmann, *Harold E. Stassen: The Life and Perennial Candidacy of the Progressive Republican* (Jefferson, NC: McFarland & Co., 2013).

6. Ron Scott Sanders, "A Thicker Jesus and Democracy," in *Justice and the Way of Jesus: Christian Ethics and the Incarnational Discipleship of Glen Stassen*, ed. David P. Gushee and Reggie L. Williams (Maryknoll, NY: Orbis Books, 2020), 137.

his 1992 book, which listed seven steps of just peacemaking, Stassen named "seek human rights and justice" as the fourth step.[7] In a 1998 multi-authored volume that he edited, he included a chapter by Bruce Russert called "Advance Democracy, Human Rights, and Religious Liberty," thus broadening the concept of just peacemaking to include democracy explicitly.[8] After that, Stassen always included "advancing democracy" as a practice of just peacemaking.

In his contribution to Stassen's 1998 *Just Peacemaking*, Russert argues from historical data that "democracies are unlikely to engage in militarized disputes with each other or to let any such disputes escalate into war."[9] The implication of Russert's finding is that if one wants international peace, one should support stable constitutional democracies. So here is the first element of Stassen's case for democracy—it contributes to peace, which is a central aspect of the common good both in national life and in international affairs. That claim can be debated in various ways, but it is a place to start in understanding Stassen's strong support for democracy. It is certainly visible today in the attack of autocratic Russia on democratic Ukraine. It is hard to imagine a democratic country initiating such a stupid, senseless, and destructive war.

Early Modern Democracy: An Innovation of Christian Dissenters

Stassen joins scholars such as Michael Walzer, Charles Taylor, and James Hastings Nichols in arguing that the modern democratic tradition began as a Christian rather than an Enlightenment-liberal innovation. It emerged from the English Puritans, chronologically

7. Glen H. Stassen, *Just Peacemaking: Transforming Initiatives for Justice and Peace* (Louisville: Westminster John Knox, 1992), 103.

8. Glen H. Stassen, ed., *Just Peacemaking: Ten Practices for Abolishing War* (Cleveland: Pilgrim Press, 1998).

9. Bruce Russert, "Advance Democracy, Human Rights, and Religious Liberty," in Stassen, ed., *Just Peacemaking*, 97.

well ahead of the writings of early Enlightenment figures like John Locke.[10] This early-modern Christian approach to democracy avoided some of the crucial errors later associated with the liberal philosophical and political tradition, such as its excessive individualism and libertarianism, and its negative stance toward religious convictions and communities.

The claim that the modern democratic tradition can be traced to an obscure wing of the English Puritan movement is an argument related to the complex history of ideas. It is *not* an endorsement of all things Puritan. As a matter of history, it appears sound, especially if the long-run trajectory is properly described. Stassen attempts this in his book *A Thicker Jesus*.[11] Here is my synopsis of Stassen's account.

The Puritans began life as a dissenting religious movement within England, calling for a thorough theological and moral reform of the Anglican Church. Their theology was Calvinist, emphasizing the sovereignty of God over all of life. They sought a genuinely rather than nominally Christian nation, governed on the basis of "biblical understandings of covenant justice."[12] The Puritans wanted to defeat the Anglican establishment, and most sought reform both of the church and of English government. Eventually, civil war and a temporarily successful proto-democratic government ensued. The Puritans gained tremendous power after their successes during the first English Civil War (1642–1646), but they were on the losing end later, after the restoration of the monarchy in 1660. The Puritans did not remain in power, but their ideas left their mark.

---

10. Stassen, *Thicker Jesus*, 64–67. Stassen's three key sources here are Michael Walzer, *The Revolution of the Saints: A Study in the Origins of Radical Politics* (Cambridge, MA: Harvard University Press, 1965); Charles Taylor, *A Secular Age* (Cambridge, MA: Belknap Press of Harvard University Press, 2007); James Hastings Nichols, *Democracy and the Churches* (New York: Greenwood, 1951).

11. Stassen, *Thicker Jesus*, ch. 5.

12. Stassen, *Thicker Jesus*, 59.

The Puritans' covenantal imagination dramatically shifted their theology of the church from what existed in Anglicanism. Michael Walzer says that Puritan churches were "formal," "voluntary," and "purposive" covenant communities.[13] Even though they understood believers to be divinely chosen for salvation, such believers freely covenanted together to undertake the rigorous way of life required of "saints." This way of life did not stop at the doors of the church. Saints were those "committed to work for God's purposes in their own lives and in society."[14]

Stassen argues that this disciplined and purposeful covenantal vision for church life "also formed a basis for the saints' calling to work for constitutional democracy."[15] At one level, because their calling was to advance the sovereign will of God in every area of life, they could not help but bring their religious vision into their engagement as citizens. Theirs was not a narrowly sectarian, church-focused vision. Further, this work was the calling of *all* covenanted believers, not just a clerical elite, thus planting the seeds of a democratic vision. The Puritans envisioned the gradual transformation of society, in part through their determined influence, so that it became more obedient to God's will. Many Calvinists today still articulate and seek to live out this kind of vision.

As early as 1620, Puritans began making their way across the Atlantic. They not only founded churches there. In New England under Puritan influence, "the settlements, towns, and states lacked models for founding themselves, so they adapted the well-known practice of church covenanting to legitimize themselves. The constitutional emphasis in American democracy thus has its roots in the covenanting practices of churches."[16] As we will consider again in chapter 14, a covenantal vision helped shape early American

13. Walzer, *Revolution of the Saints*, 317–18.
14. Stassen, *Thicker Jesus*, 64.
15. Stassen, *Thicker Jesus*, 65.
16. Stassen, *Thicker Jesus*, 73.

democratic tradition. It was not the only strand in that tradition, but it was an important one.

As any viewer of *The Crucible* would know, the Puritans had their problems. They tended toward "clerical authoritarianism," the "rage for order" (Charles Taylor's phrase), "sexual repression," patriarchalism, and dramatic "attempts to reorder whole societies" based on their ascetic religious vision.[17] The Puritan idea, as Stassen calls it, of "liberty with covenant responsibility"[18] was leached of much of its liberty, leaving authoritarian religious repression. The concept of covenant, if it was to extend to public life, needed to be corrected to admit greater acceptance of conscientious freedom, diversity, and pluralism.

These problems engendered two different forms of negative reaction, one much better known than the other. The reaction that came first was the dissenting "free-church Puritan" or post-Puritan sects that split off from the main Puritan movement. These eventually yielded all kinds of groups, including the General Baptist wing of the early Baptist movement, which also had a covenantal theological vision for the church, sometimes extended to a covenantal sensibility for the ordering of society, but a much greater sensitivity to convictional pluralism and the need for religious liberty.[19]

The reaction that came second can be summarized as Enlightenment liberalism, which emphasized human liberty, the individual pursuit of happiness, social progress rather than tradition, religious toleration but also religious skepticism, reason and science as the basis of reliable knowledge, and democratic/republican govern-

17. Stassen, *Thicker Jesus*, 59, 66.

18. Stassen, *Thicker Jesus*, 60.

19. See James Leo Garrett, *Baptist Theology: A Four-Century Study* (Macon, GA: Mercer University Press, 2009), 16–22. See also Paul S. Fiddes, William H. Brackney, and Malcolm B. Yarnell III, *The Fourth Strand of the Reformation: The Covenant Ecclesiology of Anabaptists, English Separatists, and Early General Baptists*, ed. Paul S. Fiddes (Oxford: Regent's Park College, 2018), 9–10.

ment. Enlightenment thinkers desired to weaken the role of religious traditions and institutions in public life, in part because of their association with religious intolerance and civil violence.

Walzer says that Enlightenment liberalism, in its tendency toward optimistic rationalism, somewhat lost its realism about human sin and about the need to encourage virtue and self-control among fallible people. In purposely attenuating the power of religious traditions, liberalism also fatefully weakened the sources of the citizen virtue on which social order depends.[20]

A more radical version of this argument was published in 2018 by Catholic political scientist Patrick Deneen. His claim is that classic Enlightenment liberalism contains the seeds of its own demise. After almost five hundred years, Deneen says, it appears to be an exhausted tradition, which helps to explain our current social and political crises.[21]

Deneen eerily anticipated the current situation in Western politics, at least as conservatives are describing it. That situation consists of a possible collapse of liberal democracy either into the "administrative state" imposing progressive liberalism by government fiat on the one hand, or "some form of populist nationalist authoritarianism or military autocracy" on the other.[22] This would be a post-liberal fight to the finish between two forms of illiberalism—left-liberal orthodoxy, on the one hand, and authoritarian reactionary religio-politics on the other, fighting over the carcass of liberal democracy (and culture). Progressives, of course, are quite worried about the right-wing nightmare, and conservatives believe they are already enduring the left-wing nightmare.

20. Stassen, *Thicker Jesus*, 65.
21. Patrick Deneen, *Why Liberalism Failed* (New Haven: Yale University Press, 2018). Deneen writes that the book was completed three weeks before the 2016 election (xxv).
22. Deneen, *Why Liberalism Failed*, 180-81. Another very helpful, less pessimistic take on the subject is Francis Fukuyama, *Liberalism and Its Discontents* (New York: Farrar, Straus & Giroux, 2022).

Stassen argues that both the Christian dissenters and the Enlightenment liberals created modern democracy. But the Christian contributions to early modern democratic thinking have been ignored compared to the dominant Enlightenment side. This means that we already have resources in the pre-liberal, pre-Locke period that can help us avoid the weaknesses of liberalism. The question is whether those resources can be activated before it is too late.

The tendency simply to dismiss classical (and often contemporary progressive) liberalism as irredeemable has been bad for Christian democratic participation. This tendency includes not just certain right-wing ideologues, but sophisticated contemporary theologians, among whom Stassen features the influential Duke professor Stanley Hauerwas. Especially early in his career, Hauerwas routinely suggested that Christians should be indifferent to, uninvolved in, or opposed to democracy; he linked that posture mainly to the fatal flaws of liberalism.[23] Stassen always argued that this move was wrong both as history and as Christian ethics, and that antiliberal rhetoric from influential Christian theologians was profoundly damaging to Christian democratic participation where it was most needed.

Reinhold Niebuhr was correct in this historical judgment about the mixed sources of modern democracy:

> For a long time a debate has been waged between Christian and secular leaders on the question whether democracy is the product of the Christian faith or a secular culture . . . as a matter of history, both Christian and secular forces were involved in establishing the political institutions of democracy; and the cultural resources of modern free societies are jointly furnished by both Christianity and modern secularism.[24]

23. Stassen, *Thicker Jesus*, 61–62. Stassen quotes Hauerwas's *Community of Character* (Notre Dame: University of Notre Dame Press, 1981), among other sources, while acknowledging that Hauerwas evolved somewhat in his writing on this subject.

24. *Reinhold Niebuhr on Politics: His Political Philosophy and Its Application to Our Age as Expressed in His Writings*, ed. H. R. Davis and R. C.

Glen Stassen believed, and I agree, that the disdain for democracy as merely an expression of secular Enlightenment liberalism, and the view of democracy as a matter of relative indifference in church-focused Christian ethics, have been most unfortunate developments in recent Christian thought. The trend has been influential in weakening commitment to democracy and participation in democratic reform movements.[25] Instead we should encourage *both the renewal of churches as serious covenant communities in the way of Jesus and involvement in democratic politics* in a manner "faithful to Christian ethics."[26]

The Baptist Contribution to Early Democracy

In describing precisely what democratic politics he was proposing, Stassen argued for what I call the Baptist democratic political tradition, keeping in mind that other believers' church and congregationalist groups have often held similar views. The deep Baptist contribution to early democracy was central to Stassen's pride in his Baptist identity as well as his support for democracy. Its elements are visible from Baptist origins in the early seventeenth century.

Authoritarianism was abandoned on behalf of democracy. Baptists knew the dangers of authoritarian power in both church and state. They rejected authoritarian rule in their congregations and replaced it with the lordship of Christ as expressed through the

Good (New York: Charles Scribner's Sons, 1960), 186. Quoted in Larry L. Rasmussen, ed., *Reinhold Niebuhr: Theologian of Public Life* (London: Collins, 1989), 255.

25. Stassen shows through an engagement of J. H. Yoder's "Christian Case for Democracy" that even a committed Anabaptist such as Yoder could and did make a biblical and tactical case for Christian support for democracy. *Thicker Jesus*, 70–71.

26. Stassen, *Thicker Jesus*, 62. A splendid recent work that overcomes this unfortunate and unnecessary church versus politics dualism is Luke Bretherton's magisterial work, *Christ and the Common Life: Political Theology and the Case for Democracy* (Grand Rapids: Eerdmans, 2019).

collective decisions of the faith community. They came to support political democracy for many of the same reasons. Democracy was better than autocracy in institutions of all types. The point remains relevant today.

State authority over religious belief was abandoned on behalf of religious liberty. Baptists initially fought for basic religious liberty for dissenting Christians like themselves. They then saw that the same principle also must apply to other religious minorities, including Jews and Muslims. Groups like the Baptist World Alliance still fight for religious liberty for those of non-Christian faith.[27] For Baptists then and now, this is an expression not of religious indifference but of God's absolute sovereignty over human conscience. All parties in our contemporary debates need to be reminded that when people find that their most fundamental convictions are being attacked by the state, they will fight back. Christians need to be reminded to fight for the liberty of conscience of everyone, not just us.

Removing state coercion in religion had the salutary benefit of "weaken[ing] a major cause of secularism,"[28] which is negative reaction to state-sponsored religious oppression. We have seen that resentment at work, for example, in the anticlerical fervor of the French Revolution, which initiated the spiral of secular revolution and religious counterrevolution in that country.

The establishment of a state religion was abandoned on behalf of religious disestablishment with free exercise of religion. These Baptists believed ardently that government had no legitimate role policing religious belief and suppressing minority religions. They brought this commitment into the development of democracy in the colonial and revolutionary era of the United States. It is one big reason why Virginia Baptists such as John Leland, for example, required guarantees of disestablishment and free exercise of religion before

27. "On Religious Liberty," Baptist World Alliance, https://tinyurl.com/4k9932dw.
28. Stassen, *Thicker Jesus*, 66.

they would support ratification of the US Constitution. Stassen joins others in crediting Baptists with major responsibility for the US First Amendment, which in turn was crucial to ratification of the Constitution.[29] Whether from left or right, we need to refrain from creating a "state religion."

Arbitrary government power was constrained on behalf of human rights protections. The breakthrough that government must be constrained from violating religious liberty, and that people had a right to such, eventually broadened to include commitment to a richer portfolio of rights that became essential to the development of the human rights commitments of democratic law and culture.

For one example of an early, radical, baptistic Christian making these kinds of moves, consider Richard Overton (1599–1664), a Stassen favorite. Overton was a Baptist pamphleteer and a member of the radical Leveller Movement in England during the English Civil War. In 1615 he came to the Netherlands and joined the Waterlander Mennonite Church.

In 1647 Overton published the first comprehensive Christian doctrine of human rights, which emphasized full religious liberty, a wide range of civil liberties, and rights to dignity through equal political participation without regard to sect.[30] This was almost 150 years before the US First Amendment was ratified.

Overton also included a statement of positive economic rights, including the right to free education for all and social insurance for the most vulnerable, which was centuries ahead of its time. Unfortunately, this understanding that the right to life must be un-

29. Stassen, *Thicker Jesus*, 67. For an extended defense of this claim, along with historical analysis, see Nicholas P. Miller, *The Religious Roots of the First Amendment: Dissenting Protestants and the Separation of Church and State* (Oxford: Oxford University Press, 2012).

30. Richard Overton, *An Appeal to the Free People* (London: n.p., 1647), reprinted in D. M. Wolfe, *Leveler Manifestoes of the Puritan Revolution* (New York: T. Nelson & Sons, 1944), 154ff.

derstood to include the right to the means of making a living did not make it into the US Bill of Rights and has been a contested matter ever since in US law, culture, and ethics.[31] It is one reason why economic rights—and related public policies—have been so difficult to establish here. Overton's work teaches us several things. One is that the concept of human rights is not a merely Enlightenment liberal invention. Another is that religious (and convictional) liberty is an essential human right. A third is that free-market capitalism unhindered by a vision of economic rights chews up human lives and undermines the viability of democracy.

Practicing Democracy in Church

The democracy that Baptists have supported is not just for the nation, it is also for the congregation. Indeed, it is first for the congregation. Glen Stassen's entire experience of church life—a matter of very firm commitment on his part—was in the kind of Baptist church in which the congregation governs its own affairs as a covenantal democracy.

Baptists have learned to value and to practice democracy in their congregations over more than four hundred years. This has been crucial in creating the conditions for a sustainable democracy in lands where there are plenty of Baptists and other congregationalists—or at least where democratic congregational life is socially influential. As Walzer puts it when describing the origins of congregational decision-making with the Puritans: "Congregational life was surely a training for self-government and democratic participation."[32] It has

---

31. Stassen, *Thicker Jesus*, 67–68.

32. Walzer, *Revolution of the Saints*, 301. Luke Bretherton names many other contexts of "cooperative association," such as running schools, mutual aid societies, and professional guilds, in which people learn the practice of democracy. Bretherton, *Christ and the Common Life*, 452.

remained so in many congregations, though liberal individualism has its effects here too, and one wonders how Baptist democracy will be changed by the shift to online and hybrid church practices.

A Baptist congregation is established by a group of like-minded believers in a locality who desire to create a community to practice their faith together. *It is decidedly not an individualist, social-contract-making effort.* Historically, many Baptist congregations have begun by drafting a covenant to which all members subscribe. This covenant declares the basic theological, spiritual, and moral commitments of the congregation, all situated under the lordship of Jesus Christ. It usually includes or is soon augmented by a church constitution and bylaws that contain provisions for the governance of the community. These texts are both foundational and amendable. Notice that both covenantalism and constitutionalism were part of historic Baptist practice, long before the first democratic government was birthed.

Baptist congregations, then, are democratic, implicitly or explicitly covenantal, constitutionalist communities organized for shared religious purposes. The people constitute and govern the congregation, subject to the rules they establish, which can only be amended using agreed due process. The people select and dismiss their clergy, who come and go, while the people stay. The people set and manage their own budgets. The people determine who may join the community, as well as the theological and moral boundaries of the community.

In a Baptist congregation, only Jesus can tell the congregation what to do; though, of course, the community together determines what action Jesus is directing, which is a kind of internal church political process. The congregation is under Christ's lordship but no human authority. Clergy in Baptist congregations soon learn that they are elected to serve God and the congregation under the covenantal and constitutional structure established by the community. They ought to be good leaders, but they are not dictators. If the congregation thinks they are dictators, they soon are shown the door.

Baptist congregations have been laboratories for democracy. Ordinary people have learned how to create and sustain democratic political communities in myriads of humble little congregations. They have learned how to respect dissent and convictional differences and remain together. Sure, Baptist congregations often mess up in their inner politics, falling into irrationality, pettiness, and all manner of foolish fights. But they generally learn from their mistakes and move forward. Congregations are where the Baptist democratic Christian tradition has taken flesh. Baptists have also learned through experience that their democratic practices and norms can valuably be taken into the wider community. This encourages democratic practice in society; at least, it has the potential to do so, a potential that needs to be actualized today.

In my view, it is very important that Baptist congregations remain democratic, govern themselves successfully, have some success at forming congregants in democratic norms and practices, and teach the social applicability of these norms and practices.

Today I lament the erosion of congregationalism, with certain growing tendencies toward authoritarianism, in some quadrants of Baptist and broader congregationalist Christianity. This includes, in my view, and Glen Stassen's view, the largest Baptist denomination in the world: the Southern Baptist Convention (SBC) of the United States. Significant numbers of Baptist congregations are succumbing to pastoral or denominational authoritarianism and eroding congregational democracy. They also appear to be succumbing to authoritarianism's most common problems, such as abuse of power and lack of transparency and accountability. Where congregations sacrifice their democratic politics, they are walking away from historic Baptist democratic principles. This is not just bad for these churches but may subtly weaken the contribution of their congregants to democratic norms in public life.

If Glen Stassen were with us today, he would encourage every Christian community to maximize the democratic practices possible within its tradition, and to encourage democratic best practices both in church and in society.

An Allergy to Authoritarianism, Including of Moral Majorities

Glen Stassen's support for constitutional democracy was grounded in multiple very good reasons. Democracy values all citizens, limits government/leader power, protects individual rights and conscientious minorities, promotes peace, reflects the strengths of Baptist polity, serves democratic community, and has proven sustainable over centuries.

Stassen had not a shred of nostalgia for Christendom, no cultural despair for Christian hegemony, no dreams for a world back in the past. What he had was a remarkable allergy to authoritarianisms of all types.

Authoritarian reactionary Christianity almost always yearns for renewed power *for a particular dominant Christian community that has become intertwined with national identity*—Catholicism in France, Poland, and Hungary; Russian Orthodoxy in Russia; fundamentalist evangelicalism in Brazil and the United States. Stassen was quite clear that such religious domination is morally dangerous both for the churches and for the state.

I was reminded in an odd way of the negative moral effects of being the dominant religious group through a careful recent study of the rescue of Jews in the Netherlands and Belgium by Robert Braun.[33] Using geospatial statistics and archival work, Braun discovered that Jews were more likely to be rescued by local religious minorities than by majorities. Thus, if you were Jewish and were looking for rescue, you would want to go to Catholics if you lived

33. Robert Braun, *Protectors of Pluralism: Religious Minorities and the Rescue of Jews in the Low Countries during the Holocaust* (Cambridge: Cambridge University Press, 2020).

in a Protestant-dominated region or to Protestants if you were in a Catholic-dominated region. Braun concludes that religious minority communities were less likely to be penetrated by Nazi sympathizers and were more empathetic to those targeted for persecution. I found similar results in various settings in my own study of rescuers.[34] It is hard not to draw the conclusion that being in the religious majority often has negative moral consequences. One clear effect is how it changes the meaning of religious liberty, which tends to shift from a focus on the freedom of religious minorities, like Jews, to exist and follow their consciences, to the freedom of the religious majority to live as we wish, including by discriminating against others.[35]

Stassen would not have been surprised by these findings. He saw the role of religion in public life from the religious margins. He was not a secularist, but instead a Baptist democrat, who saw that the way minority communities are treated is a central indicator of the moral health of a society. Stassen's antipathy toward authoritarian reactionary Christianity was robust. He expected all Baptists, at least, to have such antipathy, and hoped that all Christians would. Sometimes he used medical language for this: he would say that authoritarianism is a virus, and Christians are supposed to have antibodies against this virus. He was always distressed when that expectation was disappointed.

For Stassen the value of democracy and the danger of antidemocratic Christian and secular politics was obvious from morality and history. The danger of both left- and right-wing authoritarianism was written in the blood of millions in the twentieth century. The memory of those crimes was central in Stassen's ethics as it has been in mine.

34. David P. Gushee, *Righteous Gentiles of the Holocaust: Genocide and Moral Obligation*, 2nd ed. (St. Paul: Paragon House, 2003), chs. 5–6.
35. I thank Jacob Cook for this insight, via private communication with the author.

In my training, the moral preferability of democracy was clear. We discussed historic Christian support for tyrannical political ideologies, mainly in relation to Nazi Germany, but these were always treated as aberrational, a departure from Christian norms. There was never any question about the need for robust Christian participation within the democratic process, in the form of faithful, hopeful, non-coercive Christian witness.

I have shown in this book that Christian support for antidemocratic politics has not, in fact, been aberrational. It has its own long pedigree—and is on the march today. It may be that the Baptist democratic Christian vision is more of the aberration. This is a very disturbing idea.

13

The Black Christian Democratic Tradition in the United States

What is wrong with America is not its failure to make the Constitution a reality for all, but rather its belief that persons can affirm whiteness and humanity at the same time. This country was founded for whites and everything that has happened in it has emerged from the white perspective. The Constitution is white, the Emancipation Proclamation is white, the government is white, business is white, the unions are white. What we need is the destruction of whiteness.

—James Cone (1970)[1]

Black America flipped the script on a racialized democratic state to make it more perfect. It is Black people's fight that makes the United States exceptional.

—Randal Jelks (2022)[2]

1. James Hal Cone, *A Black Theology of Liberation* (Maryknoll, NY: Orbis Books, 1970), 107.
2. Randal Maurice Jelks, *Letters to Martin: Meditations on Democracy in Black America* (Chicago: Lawrence Hill Books, 2022), 98.

Democracy is vulnerable to abuse or negation at many points. One of the most obvious and most painful vulnerabilities is racism. Racism has surfaced in every case study we have considered so far. In Europe, the racial other for centuries—and sometimes still today—has been "the Jew." Eventually it also became "the Black," when some of the colonized peoples and their descendants settled in the colonizer's lands. More recently, it has been "the Muslim" or "the refugee" of whatever racial designation, though (sadly, predictably) Europeans have welcomed the lighter-skinned refugee far more readily than desperate Black and Brown refugees.

A sacred norm of democracy is citizen equality. One person, one vote. Equal representation for all. Everyone's vote counts the same. Everyone's voice matters equally. Being a citizen is what matters.

We have seen that antidemocratic (including Christian) reactionaries often have rejected such equality insofar as it overrides older cultural paradigms and power structures. Equalizing the political status of people who are not part of the majority religion, for example, long evoked negative reaction. The same is true of women, immigrants, non-property-owners, Indigenous populations, or those of ethnic backgrounds other than the majority.

America's Original Sin

The United States may offer the most pronounced example of a nation that has never been able to overcome its founding racism, and thus has never realized its democratic principles and aspirations. Overall, the United States has enjoyed remarkable democratic stability. It has never set aside its democracy for monarchy, autocracy, or a new kind of political regime. (Consider the contrast with France.) Yet this same country has been unable to arrive at a steady practice of fair, free, and full democratic participation rights on the part of those deemed non-white. Neither the Christian nor the liberal principles that helped create modern democracy are capable of being realized in a nation that is founded on racial hierarchy.[3] But the white population of the United States, as a whole, has so far not been persuaded to abandon it. Whenever steps of progress are made, white backlash is fierce.

Authoritarian reactionary Christianity in the United States and a number of other countries is deeply entangled with white racism. In the United States, white people do not generally accept that this entanglement exists. Many who do see the connection want little to do with Christianity.[4] Some of the hard-core Christian reactionaries, on the other hand, with increasing openness define Christianity in white ethno-nationalist terms.

Torrents of research from various fields today, and from authors of varied regional and racial backgrounds and identities, confirm that dangerous reactionary trends in our politics are entwined with white racism, not just economic, moral, and religious worries.

Robert Jones, in his important books *The End of White Christian America* and *White Too Long*,[5] argues that what is truly motivating the politics of conservative white Christians, including but not limited to evangelicals, is *white reaction*. It is the end of the unquestioned political, cultural, economic, and religious dominance of the United States by white Christian people that is distorting white Christian involvement in politics. For Jones, ferocious resistance to this diminution of white power opened the door to Donald Trump—that paragon of angry white cultural resentment.

3. I am grateful to Reggie Williams for this formulation, via private communication with the author.
4. I am grateful to Erica Whitaker for this formulation, via private communication with the author.
5. Robert P. Jones, *The End of White Christian America* (New York: Simon & Schuster, 2017) and *White Too Long: The Legacy of White Supremacy in American Christianity* (New York: Simon & Schuster, 2021).

Trumpism: Nothing New under the Sun

When the conversation turns to race, Black and Brown scholars in the United States point to a much longer history than the Trump era. Many scholars, such as Jemar Tisby,[6] Miguel De La Torre,[7] and Anthea Butler,[8] remind us today that white Christians chose white tyranny over democracy in supporting slavery for 250 years, in opposing emancipation and equal political participation for African Americans in the period after the Civil War, in supporting or acquiescing quietly to white Christian terrorism during the days of the Ku Klux Klan and lynching, and by opposing voting rights protections for Black Americans during the Civil Rights struggles of the 1960s and 1970s. These scholars make clear that the illiberalism and rejection of democracy so terrifying to observers today have been the daily bread of non-white people through most of US history.

That insight is also not new. The late James Cone, one of my seminary professors, articulated it in a most radical form in his 1970 book *A Black Theology of Liberation*.[9] His claim, all those years ago, is that "whiteness" rather than democracy is what rules America. This "whiteness" is not only anti-Black; it is anti-human, and it is certainly antidemocratic. Cone's fierce criticism of white racism placed him squarely within the Black resistance tradition to white supremacy. Moreover, his theological grounding for that resistance placed him squarely in the long and defiant tradition of Black Christian abolitionism and the Black Social Gospel tradition.[10] The Black

6. Jemar Tisby, *The Color of Compromise: The Truth about the American Church's Complicity in Racism* (Grand Rapids: Zondervan, 2019).

7. Miguel A. De La Torre, ed., *Faith and Reckoning after Trump* (Maryknoll, NY: Orbis Books, 2021).

8. Anthea Butler, *White Evangelical Racism: The Politics of Morality in America* (Chapel Hill: University of North Carolina Press, 2021).

9. Cone, *A Black Theology of Liberation*, 107.

10. Gary Dorrien, *The New Abolition: W. E. B. Du Bois and the Black

Christian abolitionist and Social Gospel traditions provide the impulse and the heartbeat for the Black democratic tradition in the United States—which has always been a tradition of resistance to white America's constant negations of democracy, Christianity, and Black humanity. As Luke Bretherton has written, "The longstanding black radical tradition has generated penetrating critiques of democracy in the United States. It seeks . . . a form of antiracist, radical democratic politics—or what W. E. B. Du Bois calls 'abolition democracy'—while recognizing that such a politics is almost incomprehensible within the existing order."[11]

Our White Supremacy Is Older Than Our Democracy

In speaking of "whiteness," Cone did not mean a skin color, of course. Whiteness can be described as a lens through which people view the world. But this lens is invisible to the ones using it. It is created not to be seen.[12] Thus white people generally react with incomprehension or paroxysms of rage if its existence is proposed.

Whiteness is a vision of the anthropological supremacy of white people among the world's "races," creating belief in the moral legitimacy of dominative white power in society, and legitimating practices of destruction, enslavement, subordination, and harm to those considered non-white. Whiteness is a hierarchical view of being that creates what Eddie Glaude calls a "value gap" between white people's lives and non-white people's lives. Glaude writes: "That's white supremacy without all the bluster: a set of practices informed by the fundamental belief that white people are valued more than

---

Social Gospel (New Haven: Yale University Press, 2015); Dorrien, *Breaking White Supremacy: Martin Luther King, Jr., and the Black Social Gospel* (New Haven: Yale University Press, 2018).

11. Luke Bretherton, *Christ and the Common Life: Political Theology and the Case for Democracy* (Grand Rapids: Eerdmans, 2019), 82.

12. I am grateful to Erica Whitaker, who is writing her dissertation on this theme; via private communication with the author.

others."[13] Only such a perceived hierarchy of being, only such a value gap, could make it possible for Black people to be viewed for centuries as rightly the material possession of white people.[14] And only such a value gap can explain white people's perpetuations of racist practices and attitudes today.

Whiteness, then, is a name for this evil power that damages everything that it touches, not just its non-white targets but also the souls of white people and the moral integrity of whiteness-damaged Christianity. Until whiteness, *thus defined*, is uprooted, defeated, and repented, there can be no genuine democracy in the United States. This was Cone's view in 1970, and he never really changed it. I have now come to share this view, which seemed radical to me until everything that happened in the United States from 2015 forward. It should not have taken that long, but white folks' illusions die hard.

Cone's reading of the demonic power of whiteness made revolution rather than reform his political agenda. He was not much interested in tinkering with democratic reforms because he believed that white people would always manipulate democracy to harm Black people. The ideology of whiteness must be destroyed before one can even begin to talk about reforming or perfecting democracy.

Of course, there were and are other Black perspectives on democracy. Martin Luther King Jr. articulated a very different vision. In his most optimistic-sounding articulations, as in his "I Have a Dream" speech of August 1963, he took the most famous words in the US Declaration of Independence—"We hold these truths to be self-evident, that all men are created equal, that they are endowed by their Creator with certain unalienable rights"—as applying to Black people. The issue was a failure to deliver what was promised in 1776:

13. Eddie S. Glaude Jr., *Democracy in Black: How Race Still Enslaves the American Soul* (New York: Crown Publishers, 2016), 30.
14. I am grateful to Reggie Williams for this formulation, via private communication with the author.

In a sense we've come to our nation's capital to cash a check. When the architects of our republic wrote the magnificent words of the Constitution and the Declaration of Independence, they were signing a promissory note to which every American was to fall heir. This note was a promise that all men, yes, black men as well as white men, would be guaranteed the "unalienable Rights" of "Life, Liberty and the pursuit of Happiness." It is obvious today that America has defaulted on this promissory note, insofar as her citizens of color are concerned. Instead of honoring this sacred obligation, America has given the Negro people a bad check, a check which has come back marked "insufficient funds."

Rhetorically, at least, King celebrated the democratic principles and constitutional structures of the United States, claiming that "every American" is heir to these principles and promises. He appealed to white Americans to join with "citizens of color" in helping America "live out the true meaning of her creed."

King was fully aware that this was a strategic way to frame the matter so that it could be heard and acted on by well-intentioned white people. King could have said what Randal Jelks says in his bracing 2022 book *Letters to Martin: Meditations on Democracy in Black America*:

The framers of the United States Constitution got the legalities of a democratic process partially right—right enough for them to compromise with one another and establish a racially exclusive democracy. But this was a compromise among one class of people, rather than one between all those in the new nation. They consciously, though stealthily, promoted vile enrichments from enslavement. Feverishly they employed colonial thuggery to remove Indigenous nations across North America.[15]

15. Jelks, *Letters to Martin*, 31.

Indeed, there were times when King said things just like this. But for his most important national address, King's strategy was to invite white Americans to reenvision our national heritage as containing a principle of including everyone, but a practice falling short of principle—a practice that could now be altered.

> I have a dream that one day this nation will rise up and live out the true meaning of its creed: "We hold these truths to be self-evident, that all men are created equal."

When one thinks about how long and hard Black Americans have had to fight for the most basic recognition and rights, it seems to me that they have faced a perennial fight-or-flight dilemma in the United States. They could either attempt to *flee* (spiritually, psychologically, or literally) from this country, or they could fight: for survival, for dignity, for civil rights, for justice, for democracy. Randal Jelks is right when he claims that those who did not flee, those who fought, are the true democrats in American history:

> Black histories shred the mythology of the American Revolution, Lincoln freeing the slaves, Lost Causes, and landings on Plymouth Rock. Our histories are contrapuntal. They defy the idea that people of the United States are God-fearing. If anything, it is our [Black people's] histories that are exceptional. We have been the ones that have demonstrated a commitment to being democratic.[16]

The Black Christian Struggle for Democracy

I honor the Black democratic tradition precisely in these terms.[17] I want to be sure to name the profound role of Black Christians in

16. Jelks, *Letters to Martin*, 11.
17. Two formative books for me in this vast literature are Cornel West,

leading democratic movements in this country—Black Christians who often, as noted in the last chapters, learned their democratic politics through the Baptist and other polities in which they have governed themselves. They also learned versions of Christian theology and ethics in which democratic participation for justice and dignity for all people were so often articulated. While the Black democratic tradition contains plenty of non-Christian voices—in part because white Christians have so discredited Christian faith—the Black democratic tradition has been suffused with a defiantly inclusive version of Christian faith from the very beginning of the American experience.

White Christian people have rarely had to risk their lives to participate in public debate, to protest, or to vote. It has been easy for us to take for granted what was handed to us at birth. That has never been the case for Black Americans. If we wish to understand what it takes to build, sustain, and reform a democracy, it is to this tradition, and others like it, that we all must look. Democracy must be fought for. Those who have had to claw their way into political enfranchisement fully understand.

We have thought much in this book about authoritarian reactionary Christians who thought democracy was banal and dreamed authoritarian dreams. But Jelks rightly argues that for Black Americans, at least, democracy has never been banal, and has also required faith and hope:

> In my estimate this is what democracy is all about: the breath of self-respect and respect for others. This is the truth of all great faiths—and democracy is a faith, a belief system. This is why we must consider democracy as a matter of the spirit.[18]

Democracy Matters: Winning the Fight against Imperialism (New York: Penguin Press, 2004), and Glaude, *Democracy in Black*. For the longer heritage, any reading list must include, among others, Frederick Douglass, Ida B. Wells-Barnett, W. E. B. Du Bois, Langston Hughes, James Baldwin, Angela Davis, and of course, Martin Luther King.

18. Jelks, *Letters to Martin*, 16.

I noted earlier that Paul de Lagarde and his cohort dreamed of a past that never quite existed and a future yet to be born—and that, for them, this was dangerous fantasy. And yet in a richly empowering and paradoxical way so have Black democrats dreamed of a past that never quite existed and a future yet to be born.[19] Consider Langston Hughes:

> O, let America be America again—
> The land that never has been yet—[20]

Black democrats offer an honest version of American history and a hard-won vision of America's future. All democrats would do well to listen closely.

Liberal Cynicism Has a Point—but Is It Constructive?

Many on the liberal and radical side of the United States political spectrum sound more cynical today than at any time in my lifetime. This is interesting for conservatives to know, given their certainty that left-liberal orthodoxy is happily dominating democratic public life. Indeed, in the United States these days the feel on the left is more Cone 1970 than King 1963. Who can blame people of color for looking at US democracy as a failed project, especially after Trump?

There also appears to be a generational dimension here. Faced with inheriting a country at the point of the potential collapse of democracy, and potentially irrevocable ecological devastation, and preposterous levels of economic inequality, many are defaulting to pessimism, cynicism, and escapism.[21] I would only say that

19. Discussing this issue, Bretherton cites St. Augustine: "That republic never actually existed, because there was no true justice in it." *Christ and the Common Life*, 115.

20. Cited in Jelks, *Letters to Martin*, 21.

21. I am grateful to Jacob Cook for this formulation, via private communication with the author.

cynicism about democracy probably will not help fix what is so very broken here. The idea that we never were and *never can be* anything more than a white-male-plutocrat ethnocracy, that the game is rigged against everyone else, does not encourage the fight for democracy that we need here.

If you add that liberal cynicism to the toxicities on the right, the center of gravity for an incrementally reformist democratic politics is threatened. We need a politics right now involving both retrieval of the best of the past and dramatic transformation that finally overcomes toxic whiteness. Meanwhile America's white Christians and Christianity are being weighed in the balance and found wanting. Can it be that we never really have had a genuinely democratic Christian vision in this country? Is the picture really that bad?

The Need to Embrace the Dissident Black Struggle for Democracy

This much is clear: the defense of democracy in my country today is clearly intertwined with the four-hundred-year struggle of African Americans to participate in a polity that at last includes them in the democratic covenant on equal terms. This is one path ahead toward the defense of democracy from its Christian enemies—that is, the embrace of the dissident Black Christian democratic tradition, as articulated by leading Black thinkers since the very beginning of our nation. While we do not all share the same history, all kinds of people, in the United States and around the world, can and do take inspiration from the Black struggle for true democracy. It has inspired many other movements to extend real equality to all—which, after all, is what democracy always says that it is about: "all are created equal," "liberty and justice for all," and all that. This is one reason why true democrats can never rest easy with the way authoritarian movements always seem to move toward anti-egalitarianism and to target certain groups in society as not quite worthy of full liberty and justice.

In his *The Planet You Inherit: Letters to My Grandchildren When Uncertainty's a Sure Thing*, Union Seminary ethicist Larry Rasmussen puts it this way:

> King's campaign lodges in public memory as the civil rights movement. While not wrong, it's incomplete. You'll have seen footage of the March on Washington and heard the I Have a Dream speech. But it was not the March on Washington for Civil Rights. It was the March on Washington *for Freedom and Jobs*. King's movement was unwavering that genuine democracy—freedom—is economic, political, and social, each dimension critical for the others. The three together, equally for all, is democracy fulfilled. [22]

Black historian Randal Jelks agrees:

> The civil rights movement was about the reconfiguration of democracy. What the countless known and unknown leaders like [King] did was to make a commitment to democratic political struggle, the struggle to give voice and voices to a people. [23]

The Black democratic tradition teaches us much that all Christian democrats should support: the ongoing battle for an inclusive democracy; the equal dignity and worth of all persons; the moral and legal right of everyone in society to political participation; the protection of human rights, with special focus on the mistreated, marginalized, and minoritized; the struggle for advances in economic democracy and basic economic justice; and the vigorous protection and improvement both of democratic norms and dem-

22. Larry L. Rasmussen and Terry Tempest Williams, *The Planet You Inherit: Letters to My Grandchildren When Uncertainty's a Sure Thing* (Minneapolis: Broadleaf Books, 2022).

23. Jelks, *Letters to Martin*, 156–57.

ocratic institutions. These norms and institutions are always at risk, but especially when those in power don't like the results of free and fair elections, and even more so when the decisive votes are provided by people of color that some powerful people, in their heart of hearts, think never really belonged in the first place.

Jelks writes: "Democracies the world over are troubled. However, thinking back on the history of our country, when was democracy ever fully realized? . . . American democracy has been troublesome . . . from the beginning."[24] We learn from the Black democratic tradition that if one wants democracy, this "requires a never-ending devotion to the actual building of a free and open democratic society."[25] This work often requires great sacrifice. It is never done. And it is worthy of the efforts of followers of Jesus.

24. Jelks, *Letters to Martin*, 179.
25. Jelks, *Letters to Martin*, 43.

14

Renewing the Democratic Covenant

> The body politic is formed by a voluntary association
> of individuals: it is a social compact, by which the
> whole people covenants with each citizen, and each
> citizen with the whole people.
>
> —Preamble to the Massachusetts
> Constitution (1780)[1]

Notice the word "covenant" in that preamble. The writers of
the Massachusetts Constitution express a "covenantal" understanding of democracy. This chapter will argue that one way
forward for Christians is an intentional renewal of a covenantal
understanding of democracy fit for our times. This is a Christian
approach that long precedes John Locke and liberal democratic theory, and which, I believe, can be usefully renewed today. It offers
challenges to Christians and others, along the entire political and
ideological spectrum.[2]

1. Quoted by Michael Walzer, *Exodus and Revolution* (New York: Basic
Books, 1984), 84.
2. Three helpful books that explicitly deploy the concept of covenant
to think about historic and normative Christian engagement with politics
include Luke Bretherton, *Christ and the Common Life: Political Theology
and the Case for Democracy* (Grand Rapids: Eerdmans, 2019); Marcia Pally,
*Commonwealth and Covenant: Economics, Politics, and Theology of Relation-
ality* (Grand Rapids: Eerdmans, 2016); and Philip Gorski, *American Cove-

Covenant: The Gift of the Jewish People to Our Cultures

"Covenant" is a central biblical term. Indeed, the case has been made, most recently by Christian ethicist Hak Joon Lee, that covenant is the central organizing category of Jewish and Christian theology and ethics.[3] This was the belief of many Christians in the colonial era of the future United States, and it was especially central for those in the Calvinist lineage, which included the Puritans of New England.

In Scripture, after the cataclysm of the flood, God makes a covenant with Noah and through him with humanity and the whole creation; then with Sarah and Abraham and their descendants; then with Moses and the delivered slaves after the exodus; then with David and his kingly lineage. Through the life, death, and resurrection of Jesus, all who seek to worship Israel's God and abandon their idols are included in a covenant relationship with God.

The most significant biblical covenants involve promises made both by God and by people. The relationship between divine and human is not a bond between peers, but there is always a dimension of reciprocity and voluntary decision on both sides. Most often, God is depicted as choosing to initiate a covenant with a particular group of people. The offered covenant involves behavioral expectations on both sides. The people are given a choice to commit to the covenant that God is offering, but if they assent, they are bound to its terms. Biblical covenants are sacred, mutual, and binding.[4]

When covenants are made between people in Scripture, God is often called upon as witness and guarantor. God becomes the transcendent third party in covenants between people. One can easily see how

---

nant: *A History of Civil Religion from the Puritans to the Present* (Princeton: Princeton University Press, 2017).

3. Hak Joon Lee, *Christian Ethics: A New Covenant Model* (Grand Rapids: Eerdmans, 2021). See also William Johnson Everett, *A Covenantal Imagination: Selected Essays in Christian Social Ethics* (Eugene, OR: Resource Publications, 2021).

4. Pally, *Commonwealth and Covenant.*

important this is in situations in which there is no reliable or available human guarantor of covenants. If one is going to risk much in making binding promises to others, it helps to know that all parties believe that the covenant has a vigilant, just, and powerful God as its guarantor.

The idea that the religious community should be understood as covenantal in nature was obviously central in Jewish tradition. At every stage of its history, the Jewish people understood themselves to be covenantally bound to God and each other. A tremendous advantage of this vision proved to be that it could work regardless of the nature of Jewish political sovereignty at a given time. God related to the Jewish people through covenant, whether Israel was a tribal confederation, a kingship, in exile, or returned to its land under someone else's imperial rule.

A covenantal understanding of Christian life is easily traced to the New Testament (e.g., the "New Covenant"—Luke 22:20; 1 Cor. 11:25), and we have already seen that Puritans and Baptists are among those church traditions that have centered the concept of covenant in organizing their congregations. Such covenants are made with one another and with God, and are intended, like the covenants of Scripture, to be sacred, mutual, and binding. There is nothing individualist about covenant—it is an intrinsically relational and communal concept. This concept can help correct the central weakness of liberal democratic theory. Covenants are much more than wary contracts between autonomous individuals, and healthy democracies are much more than wary agreements among rights-maximizing free agents.

There is an implicit democratizing dimension in covenantal understandings of community. Even in those cases in which God is understood as initiating a covenant, the human beings involved must say yes. They must choose to bind themselves to God and one another. They can say no. They are not merely vassals under a king. They are decision-making agents. Not only that—all the human participants in a covenant share a fundamental kind of equality. This makes covenant a promising concept to correlate with democratic citizenship.

Covenantal Politics in Early America

It should not be surprising that people whose religious formation was dominated by biblical covenantalism should think of politics in covenantal terms as well. The Puritans who left England and settled in New England carried with them an explicitly covenantal understanding of the community they were seeking to establish. They were not merely aiming for the freedom to establish churches that were covenantal in nature. They wanted to create a covenantal political community. The Puritans had been unable to prevail in doing this back in England.

And thus, the idea of covenant entered colonial American politics. Its staying power is visible in the fact that it made its way into the Massachusetts constitution over 150 years later. A close reading of the entire preamble to that state constitution shows that the religious dimension has been muted but has not entirely gone missing. Notice how talk of God shows up:

> We, therefore, the people of Massachusetts, acknowledging, with grateful hearts, the goodness of the great Legislator of the universe, in affording us, in the course of His providence, an opportunity, deliberately and peaceably, without fraud, violence or surprise, of entering into an original, explicit, and solemn compact with each other; and of forming a new constitution of civil government, for ourselves and posterity; and devoutly imploring His direction in so interesting a design, do agree upon, ordain and establish the following *Declaration of Rights, and Frame of Government*, as the CONSTITUTION OF THE COMMONWEALTH OF MASSACHUSETTS.[5]

Such language could be read by Deists and skeptics as a decorative religious addition to what amounts mainly to an Enlightenment-

---

5. "Massachusetts Constitution" (1780), accessed at https://tinyurl.com/mu92vryz.

rationalist social contract between individuals. To religious Massachusetts citizens, it could be read as something more. It reads to me like a serious democratic covenant text, with God as its witness. This was democracy as a covenant among citizens—not just democracy as a set of agreed procedures and laws, but democracy as a covenant that citizens make with one another. The Puritans were far from perfect, but they may have something to offer us here.

Time to Restore an Old Word to Service Again?

Covenant language has pretty much disappeared from public life. The only time most everyday Americans make something like a covenant vow is if they are being naturalized. Military members and some government officials also take oaths of various types. We vow to tell the truth when we testify in court. That's about it, though. We need to do a great deal more to build a sense of covenant commitment among citizens in democracies.

It is time to press for democratic *covenant renewal* in lands where democracy has for years felt like a tired inheritance rather than a vital contemporary commitment. Like any other covenant in human life, the covenant of democracy cannot be taken for granted—and it takes more than law codes and agreed procedures to sustain it. Just like with a marriage that is in trouble, it may be time to renew our democratic covenant vows.

According to Randal Jelks, as early as his seminary days, Martin Luther King had been thinking about "the meaning of a new democratic covenant" for the United States.[6] This covenant would overcome the disastrous built-in weaknesses of the original democratic covenant codified in the US Constitution. The colonists never imagined an American covenant that would extend to the descendants of the slaves "hidden in the spaces and nuanced silences of the

---

6. Randal Maurice Jelks, *Letters to Martin: Meditations on Democracy in Black America* (Chicago: Lawrence Hill Books, 2022), 74.

original wording of the Constitution,"[7] but that is precisely what Dr. King was envisioning in seminary and what the civil rights movement demanded. This was to be a new American covenant in which everyone was included—and yet old in that, as King said, the core principle of this new covenant, though unrealized, was already articulated in US founding documents.

Democracy Requires Covenant Fidelity

Randal Jelks writes: "Theoretically, citizenship in the United States is not determined by blood lineage. It is determined by allegiance. The Constitution is a blood oath, a secular assent to swear and uphold its tenets."[8] Martin Luther King was calling on all Americans to renew the US democratic covenant according to its true meaning. He and others spilled their blood because of making that call.

For King, egalitarianism and inclusivity were crucial to the kind of democratic covenant that Americans should support. This was *not* mere political correctness or "woke totalitarianism." Egalitarian and inclusivist commitments reflect a quest to make a reality the equal status of all who are part of a covenant community. Anything less than equal treatment is a violation of covenant. Those who resist the equal status and just treatment of all citizens in democratic nations signal that they do not believe that all stand equal in worth and are included in the democratic covenant.

I call for a renewal of national democratic covenantalism. This is difficult, because within many nations our bonds are weak and our ideological divisions profound. But surely there are rich resources available in many of our national traditions. Leaders should find ways to articulate national founding principles, calling their citizens beyond a merely selfish vision of the good life into a sense of covenant commitment and fidelity. Leaders also need to embody and name the kinds of virtues required to meet democratic cove-

7. Jelks, *Letters to Martin*, 74.
8. Jelks, *Letters to Martin*, 103.

nant obligations, such as self-discipline, patience, unselfishness, and humility. Major state occasions, such as inaugurations and national holidays, would be good times to do this.

Officers in various branches of government should regularly articulate their specific democratic-covenantal duties, obligations, and limits. Presidents, prime ministers, security officials, attorneys general, military leaders, governors, district attorneys, legislators, judges—all operate, or should operate, under constitutional and traditional strictures that can usefully be described as covenantal. These should be articulated in public on a regular basis. Our countries can no longer afford an inarticulate void when it comes to the covenantal virtues and responsibilities that make democracy succeed.

Luke Bretherton argues that "a liberal legal-constitutional order sets a boundary *within which* democratic politics can take place. . . . [W]hile a liberal constitutional order seeks to guarantee a basic set of freedoms, these cannot exist without the politics to forge and actualize them."[9] With his own emphasis on covenantal (or "consociational") democratic politics, Bretherton is describing what this looks like. The basic idea, which we share, is this: a certain kind of covenantal, cooperative, associational form of politics precedes and sustains formal liberal-legal constitutional government. Religious groups are one important part of that mix of associations. Liberal/constitutional government both depends upon and helps to protect the forms of human community that gave it birth. The reason

9. Bretherton, *Christ and the Common Life*, 462, italics added. His inspired treatment of covenantal, or consociational (federations of cooperative, covenanted communal associations), democratic politics is discussed on pp. 389-98. This insight connects to Tocqueville's famous examination of the crucial role of voluntary civil society organizations in advancing democracy in America. "Nothing . . . is more deserving of our attention than the intellectual and moral associations of America. . . . If men are to remain civilized, or to become so, the art of associating together must grow." *Democracy in America* (New York: New American Library, 1956), part 2, book 2, 201-2.

Christians should care about both democratic politics and its for-
malized liberal constitutional expression is because they contribute
to good and flourishing lives and communities. A simple way to say
it is this: we should care because we are called to love our neighbors.
"Politics is not merely an arena for practicing neighbor-love; it can
of itself be a form of neighbor love."[10]

A Call to Renew a Christian Commitment to Democracy

On pages 184–85 I offer a chart that summarizes the resources available from the three historic strands we have discussed. These resources can support Christian democratic participation, in a manner especially summarized in the righthand box on page 185.

Now I invite readers to look again at the chart we first encountered
at the end of chapter 3, reproduced on pages 186–87. The righthand
box on page 187 offers a summary of what authoritarian reactionary
Christian politics looks like.

Considering these charts, and our journey in this book, it seems that
two possible paths lie ahead of us. The options are clear and stark.

In negative reaction to modern cultural trends, we could embrace antidemocratic political authoritarianism. We could look for
a Christian strongman to save us. We could accept that the centralization of power and the subversion of existing constitutions and
laws is a price worth paying. We could choose to manipulate national politics to override the will of democratic majorities in God's
name if we do not like what they decide.

We could seek an official or unofficial end to the separation of
church and state. We could seek the establishment of official state
Christianity and the legal enforcement of biblical laws.

We could hunker down into a culture-wars fight to the finish
against our liberal adversaries, seeking to crush them at every
opportunity.

10. Bretherton, *Christ and the Common Life*, 41.

Christian Resources for Democratic Politics

Baptist Democratic Tradition	Black Christian Democratic Tradition
• reject authoritarianism: only Christ is Lord	• resistance tradition to white supremacism
• rejection of state religion	• lineage: abolitionism and Black Social Gospel
• God's sovereignty over human conscience	• white racism seen as antidemocratic
• support disestablishment & free exercise	• US creation of racially exclusive democracy
• limit arbitrary government power	• King's move: claim the promised equality
• establish robust human rights protections	• Black sacrificial fight for true democracy
• right to equal political participation	• Black churches as HQ for democracy
• right to life including means of making a living	• defiant Black counter-theology & ethics
• right to free education & social insurance	• real democracy as dignity/ justice for all
Baptist Congregational Life	• democracy as a faith & a matter of spirit
• church as covenant community under Jesus	• citizen equality grounds broad inclusivism
• church as training in democratic self-government	• commitment: democratic political struggle
• church as training ground for virtue	• rights as economic, social, and political
• respect for everyone's convictions/dissent	• tradition offers needed spiritual resources

Democratic Covenantal Tradition	Democratic Christian Politics
• political community as covenantal	• democratic politics taught to believers
• entered formally, purposely, voluntarily	• pro-separation of church and state
• covenants as sacred, mutual, binding	• pro-disestablishment of religion
• covenants have behavioral expectations	• goal of offering faithful Christian witness
• God as witness and guarantor of covenants	• strong/broad human rights commitments
• communal not individualist-contractarian	• strong rejection of Christian nationalism
• covenants have democratizing dimension	• religious liberty focuses on religious minorities
• covenantal egalitarianism – all stand equal	• anti-nationalist as Christ alone is Lord
• democracy as covenant among citizens	• views authoritarianism as antithetical
• places emphasis on covenant obligations	• government officials remind of covenant
• covenant holds leaders accountable	• King's "new democratic covenant" for all
• covenant virtues enable covenant fidelity	• train in / expect leaders with covenant virtues

Authoritarian Reactionary Christian Politics

Authoritarian (political)	Reactionary
• rejection/weakening of democratic rules • denial of legitimacy of opponents • toleration/encouragement of political violence • readiness to curtail civil liberties & rights • usurpation & misuse of state power by rulers lamenting lost cultural uniformity • circumvention & manipulation of law • weakening of popular sovereignty • centralization, lack of checks on power • often: paternalist/masculinist vision • authoritarian (religious-moral) • centralized power vis-à-vis religious truth • top-down structures prevail • little avenue for protest or dissent • emphasis on submission to authority • environment of intimidation may exist	• counterthrust to dramatic social changes • opposed to end of throne/altar regimes • opposed to "liberalism" & "secularism" • embattled & defiant minority spirit • posture of nostalgia & perhaps despair • discomfort with pluralism & diversity • rejection of democratic egalitarianism • effort to bend the arc of history backward • may be explicitly "counterrevolutionary" • culture wars effort to take back the nation • liberals as enemies in battle of good versus evil

Christian	Authoritarian Reactionary Christian Politics
• official church authorities	• antidemocratic politics taught to believers
• self-identified Christian populations	• anti–church/state separation
• politicians deploy Christian rhetoric	• "culture wars" must be ended via victory
• seek Christian norm-setter role in culture	• impose "biblical" or "natural" law
• seek Christian institutional power/favor	• override majorities/rights in God's name
• weakened acceptance of religious diversity	• may express as Christian nation-ism
• may turn toward open antisemitism	• may fuse with racism and xenophobia
• may turn toward anti-Muslim stance	• may fuse with nationalism/ militarism
• moral traditionalism on gender, sex, family	• often anti-LGBTQ+, anti–gender equality
• may draw upon biblical apocalypticism	• may adopt conspiracy thinking
• nation as "Christian," "chosen," or "holy land"	• may adopt holy war militancy & violence
• may be expressed heretically/ immorally	• may be aided by irreligious rightist groups

We could slide even further down the moral slope away from the spirit of Christ, embracing nationalism, militarism, and imperialism. We could reverse gains for social equality, dismissing them as woke liberalism, and return to old patterns of racism, sexism, xenophobia, and contempt for LGBTQ+ people.

We could fire ourselves up about a battle of good versus evil—maybe not just a cold war of culture but a hot war of guns, in the name of our holy God.

We could decide that the gentle virtues taught by Jesus must be suspended in such a time as this. We could also choose to embrace ungodly co-combatants if they can help us win this fight.

Or, we can reject this path of authoritarian reactionary Christianity.

We can remember that Jesus Christ is Lord, and that for Christians the way of Christ does not get suspended in what we perceive, with our oh-so-limited perspective, to be emergencies.

We can recall the pro-democratic resources in Scripture. These include, at a minimum: the Genesis teaching that God is Creator and sovereign over all, and that all humans are made in God's image but also damaged by sin (Gen. 1-3); the covenantal tradition that begins between God and Noah and through him flows to all creation and all nations (Gen. 11); the Jewish covenantal tradition that follows, and extends through the rest of the Bible; the Jewish legal tradition with its covenantalism and special attention to create laws to protect the most vulnerable, like widows, orphans, aliens, and strangers; the prophetic tradition of social justice and the prophetic promise of a transformed creation; and the life, teaching, and example of Jesus, his message of the kingdom of God, the concept of the lordship of Christ, and the example offered by the radically egalitarian communities of Christians presented and addressed in the rest of the New Testament.

We can reconnect with the five-hundred-year-old democratic strands of the Christian tradition, such as the three we have considered here: congregational democracy, Black Christian democratic struggle, and democratic covenantalism.

We can reject authoritarianism because we know that God is against tyranny. We can reject it because we know that people are sinful and too much power is too strong a temptation. We may grow weary with democratic inefficiencies, struggles, and wrong turns, but authoritarianism is a siren song to be resisted.

We can remember how bad it was when religious majorities were able to impose their beliefs in violation of the consciences of dissenters, sometimes at the point of a sword or gun. Knowing how important our faith and morality are to us, we can both ask for respect for our convictions and refrain from trampling on the convictions of others.

We can learn to accept living in societies with profound diversity of belief. We can even ask God to show us what we might learn from people of other beliefs whom we encounter. We do not need cultural uniformity to practice our way of life.

We can remember the Bible's constantly articulated concern for those on the margins, those dominated by others, and we can choose not to support a politics of domination and marginalization, but instead one of dignity, equality, and justice for all.

We can remember what happened to the Old Testament prophets, John the Baptist, Jesus, and the apostles, at the hands of authoritarian rulers answerable only to themselves, and then recall why setting enforceable limits on state power over freedom and life was a breathtaking advance that must be protected.

We can renew our commitment to the political, civil, social, and economic rights of our fellow citizens, as an expression of our recognition of how much God loves and values all people. While we may not accept the legitimacy of everybody's claims to this or that supposed right, we can begin with a tender regard for the needs and rights of all our neighbors.

We can recommit to robust church participation and training in virtue, knowing that our societies need mature citizens trained in compassion, responsibility, service, honesty, and wisdom.

We can commit to a covenantal understanding of democracy, with civic participation, advocacy for the common good, and a struggle for true democracy, rather than simply retreating to our private enclaves.

We can stand against deteriorations of Christian identity such as Christian-tinged nationalism, militarism, racism, sexism, xenophobia, and contempt for LGBTQ+ people.

We can stand against the idea that the exigencies of any given moment somehow suspend basic Christian behavioral obligations like kindness, honesty, and compassion.

We can draw on the spiritual resources available to us through union with Christ to renew our service to our neighbors through democratic participation, even when there seems to be little immediate hope.

We can commit to a renewed practice of public witness to Christian values, without seeking to impose them on others. We can dream of God's reign, the transformation of the world, and do our little bit to move society forward, one day at a time. We confess that Jesus Christ is Lord, and we thank God that in democracies we are free to live this way every day. Let us do so.

A Final Word

During the Cold War, Reinhold Niebuhr wrote:

> Democracy cannot be the final end of life. . . . It is a form of human society, and man is only partly fulfilled in his social relations. Ultimately each individual faces not society but God as his judge and redeemer. . . . Democracy is certainly a better form of society than totalitarianism. But many proponents of it share one mistake of communists at least: they know of no other dimension of existence except the social one.[11]

11. *Reinhold Niebuhr on Politics: His Political Philosophy and Its Application to Our Age as Expressed in His Writings*, ed. H. R. Davis and R. C. Good (New York: Charles Scribner's Sons, 1960), 191, cited in Larry L. Ras-

Democracy, while flawed, still appears to be the best available political ordering of human community. It is not the final end of life. That ultimate destiny is eternal communion with God. And yet here on this earth democracy is still worth our support—even, if necessary, by defending democracy from its Christian enemies.

mussen, ed., *Reinhold Niebuhr: Theologian of Public Life* (London: Collins, 1989), 257.

Discussion Questions

Chapter 1: Defining and Defending Democracy

1. Discuss the idea that modern democracy consists of a combination of the rule of the people and the rule of law. What happens if one or the other is missing?
2. Is law legitimate just because legislators have decided it, or must law fit with transcendent moral principles?
3. Does a well-functioning society need a shared vision of the common good? If so, what is the role of government in helping nurture that vision?
4. Is the Freedom House list of democratic political rights and civil liberties compelling? Which rights and liberties seem most vulnerable in your country?

Chapter 2: Alternatives and Threats to Democracy

1. How was ancient Israel's connection of religion and politics different from most other countries in the ancient world?
2. Considering the definition of political authoritarianism, is your country moving toward or away from it?
3. Is left-liberal illiberal authoritarianism a reality? If so, where is it visible?

Chapter 3: Authoritarian Reactionary Christianity

1. If you are a Christian, would you describe your church community as more authoritarian or more democratic in its practices? Give examples.
2. Are the Christians that you know generally positive or negative about contemporary social changes? Is it fair to describe conservative Christians as taking a "reactionary" posture?
3. Consider Christian nationalism, religious nationalism, and Christian right-wing populism, and compare them to authoritarian reactionary Christianity. Which of these categories seems most helpful in explaining what is going on today?

Chapter 4: Secular Revolutions and Religious Counterrevolutions

1. Does the paradigm of secular revolution and religious counterrevolution accurately describe past or current political dynamics in your country?
2. How is apocalyptic thinking connected to religious counterrevolutionary efforts?
3. Is it fair to describe the founding US vision as a secular state with religious freedom? If so, is that original arrangement threatened today?

Chapter 5: Reactionary Politics in France, 1870–1944

1. How did the dynamics of secular revolution/religious counterrevolution weaken democracy in France?
2. What was the impact of the convergence of ultra-conservative Catholic religion and politics in France on the politics of the country—and on the reputation of the church?
3. "One thing worse than frankly Christian reactionary politics is its less scrupulous post-Christian, quasi-Christian, or corrupted Christian successor." Discuss.

*Chapter 6: The Politics of Cultural Despair in Germany,
1853–1933*

1. Discuss the unique, and uniquely dangerous, power of a "reactionary-utopian" ideology.
2. How did frustrated hopes of social unity, and the constant conflicts of democratic politics, deepen the politics of cultural despair in Germany?
3. How did the weakening of Christian faith in Germany prepare the way for Germanic quasi Christianity and its toxic politics?

*Chapter 7: Authoritarian Reactionary Christianity
in Putin's Russia*

1. Try to piece together the argument that the Russian invasion of Ukraine was justified by gay-pride parades.
2. Discuss the combination of nationalism, imperialism, mysticism, and morality in fueling the partnership of Putin and the Russian Orthodox Church.
3. Why are so many Christians convinced that maintaining a Christian nation is more important than democracy?

*Chapter 8: Authoritarian Reactionary Christianity
in the Recent Politics of Poland*

1. How is the European Union a player in the internal religious politics of Poland? What can be learned from this?
2. How and why is anti-LGBTQ+ propaganda used for authoritarian reactionary Christian politics? Discuss the quotation from Legutko.
3. How is the legacy of John Paul II at play, and at stake, in the current Polish political situation?

*Chapter 9: Authoritarian Reactionary Christianity
in Orbán's Hungary*

1. What is to be learned from the career trajectory of Viktor Orbán?
2. What are the most significant ways the Orbán regime has weakened democracy? Can there be such a thing as an illiberal democracy?
3. Why has Orbán become a global Christian superstar? What are the implications of this?

*Chapter 10: Authoritarian Reactionary Christianity
in Bolsonaro's Brazil*

1. Discuss how Jair Bolsonaro combines a Catholic and evangelical appeal, and constituency. What does this say about the significance of older denominational distinctions in this culture-wars era?
2. What is the significance of the claim that Brazil's evangelicals have been practicing an essentially self-interested, even corrupt, politics?
3. What is the significance of the partnership between Bolsonaro and Trump, and their families?

*Chapter 11: Authoritarian Reactionary Christianity
in Trump's United States*

1. Discuss the rhetorical moves in the insurrection-eve speech by US pastor Greg Locke. What themes do you notice?
2. What are the most significant elements of democratic backsliding in the United States?
3. Is the distinction between "democracy" and "republic" actually significant in US governance? Why is this discussion happening?

Chapter 12: The Baptist Democratic Tradition

1. Discuss the differences between early Christian democratic thinking and the paradigm offered by Locke. Do you agree that Western democracy reflects both types of influences?
2. How does democratic church practice contribute to national political democracy?
3. What do you make of the suggestion that being a dominant religious group in a society can have negative moral effects, and that early Baptist support for democracy is definitely related to Baptists' marginal status in society?

Chapter 13: The Black Christian Democratic Tradition in the United States

1. Will it require the "destruction of whiteness" (Cone) for American society to be redeemed? Or should the goal be the incremental reform of democracy?
2. What is added by framing the problem we are facing today (perhaps in several countries) as *white* authoritarian reactionary Christianity?
3. What can be learned from the centuries of arduous, costly Black American, often Christian, struggle for true democracy in the United States?

Chapter 14: Renewing the Democratic Covenant

1. What does the discovery of covenant language in early America contribute to current thinking about democratic renewal? Is the cultural gap between that era and ours too great to bridge?
2. What do you think of the idea that government officials in democracies should consciously deploy covenant language to describe their responsibilities?

3. Discuss the reasons offered for a renewal of Christian commitment to democracy. Are these persuasive? Which ones are especially important?
4. Can democracy be saved from its Christian enemies?

Works Cited

Applebaum, Anne. *Twilight of Democracy: The Seductive Lure of Authoritarianism*. New York: Anchor Books, 2021.

Appleby, R. Scott. *The Ambivalence of the Sacred: Religion, Violence, and Reconciliation*. Lanham, MD: Rowman & Littlefield, 2000.

Barreto, Raimundo, and João Chaves. "Christian Nationalism Is Thriving in Bolsonaro's Brazil." *Christian Century*, December 1, 2021, 22–25.

Bash, Dana, Jake Tapper, and Jeremy Herb. "January 6 Vice Chair Cheney Said Trump Had a 'Seven-Part Plan' to Overturn the Election. Here's What She Meant." CNN, June 10, 2022. https://tinyurl.com/3ejteceb.

"The Battle for Brazil." *Economist*, April 2, 2022.

Beres-Deak, Rita. "What Is the Hungarian 'Pedophilia Act' and What Is Behind It?" *Lefteast*, June 16, 2021. https://tinyurl.com/3yvuay9s.

Board, Riley. "College Braces for Right-Wing Speaker Accused of Homophobia." *Middlebury Campus*, April 16, 2019. https://tinyurl.com/ypdps8dd.

Bouie, Jamelle. "Expanding Democracy Is the Solution." *New York Times*, June 5, 2022, SR9.

Braun, Robert. *Protectors of Pluralism: Religious Minorities and the Rescue of Jews in the Low Countries during the Holocaust*. Cambridge: Cambridge University Press, 2020.

"Brazil: Bolsonaro Threatens Democratic Rule." *Human Rights Watch*, September 15, 2021. https://tinyurl.com/54cuptjk.

Bretherton, Luke. *Christ and the Common Life: Political Theology and the Case for Democracy*. Grand Rapids: Eerdmans, 2019.

———. *Christianity and Contemporary Politics*. Chichester, UK: Wiley-Blackwell, 2010.

———. *Resurrecting Democracy: Faith, Citizenship, and the Politics of a Common Life*. Cambridge: Cambridge University Press, 2015.

Brown, Frederick. *The Embrace of Unreason: France, 1914–1940*. New York: Anchor Books, 2014.

———. *For the Soul of France: Culture Wars in the Age of Dreyfus*. New York: Anchor Books, 2010.

Bucher, Rainer. *Hitler's Theology: A Study in Political Religion*. Translated by Rebecca Pohl. London: Continuum, 2011.

Burgess, John P. "Orthodoxy and Identity." *Christian Century*, March 23, 2022, 10–11.

Butler, Anthea. *White Evangelical Racism: The Politics of Morality in America*. Chapel Hill: University of North Carolina Press, 2021.

Cafiero, Giorgio. "Analysis: Ukraine War Has Both Blindsided and Empowered Orbán." *Al Jazeera*, June 27, 2022. https://tinyurl.com/kj7aay7r.

Caldwell, Christopher. "Poland against the Progressives." *Claremont Review of Books*, Winter 2021/2022, 34–39.

Cone, James Hal. *A Black Theology of Liberation*. Maryknoll, NY: Orbis Books, 1970.

"Conservative Political Action Conference, Hungarian Prime Minister Viktor Orbán Remarks." C-Span, August 4, 2022. https://tinyurl.com/yckysh2m.

Continetti, Matthew. *The Right: The Hundred Year War for American Conservatism*. New York: Basic Books, 2022.

"The Cross on the Ballot." *Economist*, May 14, 2022, 29–30.

"The Cult of War." *Economist*, March 26, 2022, 17–19.

De La Torre, Miguel A., ed. *Faith and Reckoning after Trump*. Maryknoll, NY: Orbis Books, 2021.

Deneen, Patrick. *Why Liberalism Failed*. New Haven: Yale University Press, 2018.

Diamond, Jeremy. "Trump: I Could 'Shoot Somebody and I Wouldn't Lose Voters.'" *CNN*, January 24, 2016. https://tinyurl.com/tt9jzn8j.

Dias, Elizabeth. "The Far-Right Christian Quest for Power: 'We Are Seeing Them Emboldened.'" *New York Times*, July 8, 2022. https://tinyurl.com/2p82uj5j.

Doerfler, Ryan D., and Samuel Moyn. "Liberals Need to Change the Rules." *New York Times*, August 21, 2022, SR9.

Dorrien, Gary. *Breaking White Supremacy: Martin Luther King, Jr., and the Black Social Gospel*. New Haven: Yale University Press, 2018.

———. *The New Abolition: W. E. B. Du Bois and the Black Social Gospel*. New Haven: Yale University Press, 2015.

———. *Social Democracy in the Making: Political and Religious Roots of European Socialism*. New Haven: Yale University Press, 2019.

———. *Soul in Society: The Making and Renewal of Social Christianity*. Minneapolis: Fortress, 1995.

Douthat, Ross. "Does Liberalism Need a Wolf at the Door?" *New York Times*, April 10, 2022, SR9.

———. "How Roe Warped the Republic." *New York Times*, May 8, 2022, SR9.

Draper, Robert. "The Arizona Experiment." *New York Times Magazine*, August 21, 2022, 42–47.

Dreher, Rod. *The Benedict Option: A Strategy for Christians in a Post-Christian Nation*. New York: Sentinel, 2017.

Eberstadt, Mary. "What the Nurses Knew." *National Review*, August 1, 2022, 20–22.

Ericksen, Robert P., and Susannah Heschel, eds. *Betrayal: German Churches and the Holocaust*. Minneapolis: Augsburg Fortress, 1999.

Everett, William Johnson. *A Covenantal Imagination: Selected Essays in Christian Social Ethics*. Eugene, OR: Resource Publications, 2021.

The Federalist Papers. No. 10. New York: Signet Classic Edition, 1999.

Fiddes, Paul S., William H. Brackney, and Malcolm B. Yarnell III. *The Fourth Strand of the Reformation: The Covenant Ecclesiology of*

Anabaptists, English Separatists, and Early General Baptists. Edited by Paul S. Fiddes. Oxford: Regent's Park College, 2018.

Finchelstein, Federico. *A Brief History of Fascist Lies*. Oakland: University of California Press, 2020.

Foa, Roberto Stefan, and Yascha Mounk. "The Signs of Deconsolidation." *Journal of Democracy* 28, no. 1 (January 2017): 5–16. https://tinyurl.com/meatpzy.

Freedom House. "Expanding Freedom and Democracy." https://tinyurl.com/yj83mtnx.

French, David. "Christian Political Ethics Are Upside Down." *Dispatch*, August 21, 2022. https://tinyurl.com/ypt66jvk.

Fukuyama, Francis. *Liberalism and Its Discontents*. New York: Farrar, Straus & Giroux, 2022.

Gallaher, Carolyn, and Garret Martin. "Viktor Orbán's Use and Misuse of Religion Serves as a Warning to Western Democracies." American University, October 27, 2020. https://tinyurl.com/3tywskww.

Garland, Robert. "Athenian Democracy: An Experiment for the Ages." Chantilly, VA: Teaching Company, 2018.

Garrett, James Leo. *Baptist Theology: A Four-Century Study*. Macon, GA: Mercer University Press, 2009.

Glaude, Eddie S., Jr. *Democracy in Black: How Race Still Enslaves the American Soul*. New York: Crown Publishers, 2016.

Gorski, Philip. *American Covenant: A History of Civil Religion from the Puritans to the Present*. Princeton: Princeton University Press, 2017.

Gorski, Philip S., and Samuel L. Perry. *The Flag and the Cross: White Christian Nationalism and the Threat to American Democracy*. New York: Oxford University Press, 2022.

Gushee, David P. *After Evangelicalism: The Path to a New Christianity*. Louisville: Westminster John Knox, 2020.

——. *Changing Our Mind*. 3rd ed. Canton, MI: Read the Spirit Books, 2019.

——. *The Righteous Gentiles of the Holocaust: Genocide and Moral Obligation*. 2nd ed. St. Paul: Paragon House, 2003.

———. *Still Christian: Following Jesus Out of American Evangelicalism*. Louisville: Westminster John Knox, 2017.

Gushee, David P., and Glen H. Stassen. *Kingdom Ethics: Following Jesus in Contemporary Context*. 2nd ed. Grand Rapids: Eerdmans, 2016.

Haidt, Jonathan. "After Babel: How Social Media Dissolved the Mortar of Society and Made America Stupid." *Atlantic*, May 2022, 56–66.

Hauerwas, Stanley. *A Community of Character*. Notre Dame: University of Notre Dame Press, 1981.

Hirschman, Albert O. *The Rhetoric of Reaction*. Cambridge, MA: Belknap Press of Harvard University Press, 1991.

Hochman, Nate. "The Doctrine of the Irreligious Right." *New York Times*, June 5, 2022, SR4–5.

Homans, Charles. "'Stop the Steal' Forever." *New York Times Magazine*, July 24, 2022, 22–31, 46–49.

Hungarian Civil Liberties Union. "Harassment of NGOs Was Ordered by Hungarian Prime Minister." *Liberties*, October 10, 2016. https://tinyurl.com/yn3dzv9x.

Ingersoll, Julie J. *Building God's Kingdom: Inside the World of Christian Reconstruction*. Oxford: Oxford University Press, 2015.

Jelks, Randal Maurice. *Letters to Martin: Meditations on Democracy in Black America*. Chicago: Lawrence Hill Books, 2022.

Jones, Robert P. *The End of White Christian America*. New York: Simon & Schuster, 2017.

———. *White Too Long: The Legacy of White Supremacy in American Christianity*. New York: Simon & Schuster, 2021.

Judis, John B. *The Populist Explosion: How the Great Recession Transformed American and European Politics*. New York: Columbia Global Reports, 2016.

Juergensmeyer, Mark. *God at War: A Meditation on Religion and Warfare*. New York: Oxford University Press, 2020.

———. *Terror in the Mind of God: The Global Rise of Religious Violence*. Berkeley: University of California Press, 2000.

"Jupiter Waning." *Economist*, June 25, 2022, 51–52.

Kazin, Michael. *The Populist Persuasion: An American History*. New York: Basic Books, 1995.

Kertzer, David I. *The Popes against the Jews: The Vatican's Role in the Rise of Modern Anti-Semitism*. New York: Alfred A. Knopf, 2001.

Kimball, Charles. *When Religion Becomes Evil: Five Warning Signs*. New York: HarperCollins, 2003.

Kirby, Alec, David G. Dalin, and John F. Rothmann. *Harold E. Stassen: The Life and Perennial Candidacy of the Progressive Republican*. Jefferson, NC: McFarland & Co., 2013.

Koyzis, David T. *Political Visions and Illusions: A Survey and Critique of Contemporary Ideologies*. Downers Grove, IL: InterVarsity Press, 2003.

Lamoreaux, Jeremy W., and Lincoln Flake. "The Russian Orthodox Church, the Kremlin, and Religious (Il)liberalism in Russia." *Palgrave Communications* 4, no. 115 (2018). https://tinyurl.com/3yx4j6e3.

Langworth, Richard. "Churchill's 'Democracy Is the Worst Form of Government . . .'" richardlangworth.com, June 20, 2022. https://tinyurl.com/rvjsmy56.

Lee, Hak Joon. *Christian Ethics: A New Covenant Model*. Grand Rapids: Eerdmans, 2021.

Legutko, Ryszard. *The Demon in Democracy: Totalitarian Temptations in Free Societies*. Translated by Teresa Adelson. New York: Encounter Books, 2018.

"The Less Accused." *Economist*, November 20, 2021, 78–79.

Levitsky, Steven, and Daniel Ziblatt. *How Democracies Die*. New York: Broadway Books, 2018.

Locke, John. *Two Treatises of Government*. Edited by Peter Laslett. New York: New American Library, 1960.

Marantz, Andrew. "The Illiberal Order." *Atlantic*, July 4, 2022, 36–47.

Marion, Jean-Luc. *A Brief Apology for a Catholic Moment*. Translated by Stephen E. Lewis. Chicago: University of Chicago Press, 2021.

"Massachusetts Constitution" (1780). https://tinyurl.com/mu92vryz.

Works Cited

Maynor, John. "Civic Republicanism." Brittanica. https://tinyurl.com/mpscr7sj.

McElroy, Robert W. "Keep Talking." *America*, July/August 2022, 22-28.

McGreevy, John. "'Natural Enemies' No More." *Commonweal*, July/August 2022, 24-28.

"Might Bolsonaro Try to Steal the Vote?" *Economist*, July 16, 2022, 32-34.

Miller, Nicholas P. *The Religious Roots of the First Amendment: Dissenting Protestants and the Separation of Church and State*. Oxford: Oxford University Press, 2012.

Miller, Paul D. *The Religion of American Greatness: What's Wrong with Christian Nationalism*. Downers Grove, IL: InterVarsity Press, 2022.

Mudde, Cas, and Cristóbal Rovira Kaltwasser. *Populism: A Very Short Introduction*. New York: Oxford University Press, 2017.

Nichols, James Hastings. *Democracy and the Churches*. New York: Greenwood, 1951.

Niebuhr, Reinhold. *The Children of Light and the Children of Darkness*. New York: Scribner's, 1944.

Nugent, Ciara. "Lula the Redeemer." *Time*, May 23/30, 2022, 66-71.

O'Malley, John W. "Papal Upgrades." *America*, July/August 2022, 39-41.

Overton, Richard. *An Appeal to the Free People* (London: n.p., 1647). Reprinted in D. M. Wolfe, *Leveler Manifestoes of the Puritan Revolution*. New York: T. Nelson & Sons, 1944.

Pally, Marcia. *Commonwealth and Covenant: Economics, Politics, and Theology of Relationality*. Grand Rapids: Eerdmans, 2016.

———. *White Evangelicals and Right-Wing Populism: How Did We Get Here?* London: Routledge, 2022.

Pan, Jovem. "Defender of the Dictatorship, Jair Bolsonaro Reinforces Controversial Phrase, 'The Mistake Was to Torture and Not to Kill.'" *Jovem Pan News*, July 8, 2016. https://tinyurl.com/39jac8fe.

"Patriarchal Sermon in the Week of Cheese after the Liturgy in the Cathedral of Christ the Savior." March 6, 2022. https://tinyurl.com/bdfjfdvu.

Pawlak, Justyna, and Alicja Ptak. "As Poland's Church Embraces Politics, Catholics Depart." Reuters, February 3, 2021. https://tinyurl.com/24bjn7de.

Petrova, Tsveta, and Senem Aydin-Düzgit. "Democracy Support without Democracy: The Cases of Turkey and Poland." Carnegie Endowment for International Peace, January 5, 2021. https://tinyurl.com/6mt2zuhb.

Phayer, Michael. *The Catholic Church and the Holocaust, 1930–1965*. Bloomington: Indiana University Press, 2000.

Poewe, Karla. *New Religions and the Nazis*. New York: Routledge, 2006.

"The Poles' Position." *Economist*, July 2, 2022, 47.

Pope Pius IX. The "Syllabus of Errors." Appendix to the papal encyclical *Quanta Cura*. https://tinyurl.com/4cws59vv.

Prange, Astrid. "Of Popes and Politicians." *Deutsche Welle*, July 24, 2017. https://tinyurl.com/2kt7cusu.

Rakove, Jack N. "What Remains of Thomas Jefferson?" *Wall Street Journal*, July 2–3, 2022, C1–2.

Rasmussen, Larry L., ed. *Reinhold Niebuhr: Theologian of Public Life*. London: Collins, 1989.

Rasmussen, Larry L., and Terry Tempest Williams. *The Planet You Inherit: Letters to My Grandchildren When Uncertainty's a Sure Thing*. Minneapolis: Broadleaf Books, 2022.

Redden, Elizabeth. "Hungary Officially Ends Gender Studies Programs." *Inside Higher Ed*, October 17, 2018. https://tinyurl.com/3a25vbu6.

Rice, Andrew. *The Year That Broke America*. New York: HarperCollins, 2022.

Roberts, Sam. "Gary North, Apostle of Bible-Based Economics, Dies." *New York Times*, March 4, 2022. https://tinyurl.com/4knmx22p.

Rocca, Francis X. "'Russian World' Is the Civil Religion behind Putin's War." *Wall Street Journal*, March 19–20, 2022, C3.

Russert, Bruce. "Advance Democracy, Human Rights, and Religious Liberty." In *Just Peacemaking: Ten Practices for Abolishing War*, edited by Glen H. Stassen. Cleveland: Pilgrim Press, 1998.

"Russia's New Era of Repression." *The Economist*, November 13-19, 2021, 15.

Sanders, Ron Scott. "A Thicker Jesus and Democracy." In *Justice and the Way of Jesus: Christian Ethics and the Incarnational Discipleship of Glen Stassen*, edited by David P. Gushee and Reggie L. Williams. Maryknoll, NY: Orbis Books, 2020.

Sanders, Ron Scott, and Scotty McLennan. *After the Election: Prophetic Politics in a Post-Secular Age*. Eugene, OR: Wipf & Stock, 2018.

Savage, John. "The John Birch Society Is Back." *Politico Magazine*, July 16, 2017. https://tinyurl.com/mr3d7jbz.

Scheppele, Kim Lane. "In Hungary, Orbán Wins Again—Because He Has Rigged the System." *Washington Post*, April 7, 2022. https://tinyurl.com/bdh5s2nd.

Schmucker, Leslie. "What Is a Principle Approach School?" Dayspring Christian Academy. https://tinyurl.com/pw56h3f4.

Seidel, Andrew. "Events, People, and Networks Leading Up to January 6." In "Christian Nationalism and the January 6 Insurrection." Baptist Joint Committee, February 9, 2022. https://tinyurl.com/3zv36j92.

Senior, Jennifer. "American Rasputin." *Atlantic*, July/August 2022, 22-35.

Shah, Timothy Samuel. Preface to *Evangelical Christianity and Democracy in Latin America*. Edited by Paul Freston. Oxford: Oxford University Press, 2008.

Shortall, Sarah. *Soldiers of God in a Secular World: Catholic Theology and Twentieth-Century French Politics*. Cambridge, MA: Harvard University Press, 2021.

Smith, Gregory A. "More White Americans Adopted Than Shed Evangelical Label during Trump Presidency, Especially His Supporters." Pew Research Center, September 15, 2021. https://tinyurl.com/2h2sd55b

Snyder, Timothy. *On Tyranny: Twenty Lessons from the Twentieth Century*. London: Bodley Head, 2017.

Solberg, Mary M. *A Church Undone: Documents from the German Christian Faith Movement*. Minneapolis: Fortress, 2015.

"Speech by Prime Minister Viktor Orbán at the 31st Bálványos Sum-

mer Free University and Student Camp." July 23, 2022. https://
tinyurl.com/dd8bdy9j.

Spike, Justin. "Hungarian Nationalist PM to Deliver Speech at CPAC."
Associated Press, July 11, 2022. https://tinyurl.com/38unurks.

Stanley, Jason. *How Fascism Works: The Politics of Us and Them*. New
York: Random House, 2020.

Stassen, Glen H. *Just Peacemaking: Transforming Initiatives for Justice
and Peace*. Louisville: Westminster John Knox, 1992.

———. *A Thicker Jesus: Incarnational Discipleship for a Secular Age*. Louisville: Westminster John Knox, 2012.

Stassen, Glen H., ed. *Just Peacemaking: Ten Practices for Abolishing War*.
Cleveland: Pilgrim Press, 1998.

Steigmann-Gall, Richard. *The Holy Reich: Nazi Conceptions of Christianity, 1919–1945*. Cambridge: Cambridge University Press, 2003.

Stephens, Bret. "I Was Wrong about Trump Voters." *New York Times*,
July 24, 2022, SR4.

Stern, Fritz. *The Politics of Cultural Despair: A Study in the Rise of the Germanic Ideology*. Berkeley: University of California Press, 1961.

Sternhell, Zeev. *Neither Right nor Left: Fascist Ideology in France*.
Translated by David Maisel. Princeton: Princeton University
Press, 1986.

Stetler, Harrison. "Catholics for Zemmour." *Commonweal*, April 2022,
14–16.

Stout, Jeffrey. *Blessed Are the Organized: Grassroots Democracy in America*. Princeton: Princeton University Press, 2012.

———. *Democracy and Tradition*. Princeton: Princeton University Press,
2004.

Stroop, Chrissy. "Putin Wants God (or at Least the Church) on His
Side." *Foreign Policy*, September 10, 2018. https://tinyurl.com/
54fy4xyb.

Suliman, Adela, and Timothy Bella. "GOP Rep. Boebert: 'I'm Tired of
This Separation of Church and State Junk.'" *MSN*, June 28,
2022. https://tinyurl.com/bdzf9fk4.

Swaim, Barton. "'America's Philosopher' Review." *Wall Street Journal*, August 5, 2022. https://tinyurl.com/292nthch.

Szelényi, Zsuzsanna. "How Viktor Orbán Built His Illiberal State." *New Republic*, April 5, 2022. https://tinyurl.com/4hd6kmcs.

Taylor, Charles. *A Secular Age*. Cambridge, MA: Belknap Press of Harvard University Press, 2007.

Tocqueville, Alexis de. *Democracy in America*. New York: New American Library, 1956.

Trofimov, Yaroslav. "How Far Do Russia's Imperial Ambitions Go?" *Wall Street Journal*, June 25-26, 2022, C1-C2.

"Vaccinated against Viktor." *Economist*, April 9, 2022, 42.

Vermeule, Adrian. *Common Good Constitutionalism*. Cambridge: Polity Press, 2022.

Walker, Shaun. "Hungarian Journalists Targeted with Pegasus Spyware to Sue State." *Guardian*, January 28, 2022. https://tinyurl.com/5da25paz.

Walsh, Molly. "Middlebury College Cancels Forum Featuring Conservative Polish Leader." *Seven Days Vermont*, April 17, 2019. https://tinyurl.com/29tshhcx.

Walzer, Michael. *Exodus and Revolution*. New York: Basic Books, 1984.

———. *In God's Shadow: Politics in the Hebrew Bible*. New Haven: Yale University Press, 2012.

———. *The Paradox of Liberation: Secular Revolutions and Religious Counterrevolutions*. New Haven: Yale University Press, 2015.

———. *The Revolution of the Saints: A Study in the Origins of Radical Politics*. Cambridge, MA: Harvard University Press, 1965.

West, Cornel. *Democracy Matters: Winning the Fight against Imperialism*. New York: Penguin Press, 2004.

Whitehead, Alfred North. *Symbolism: Its Meaning and Effect*. New York: Fordham University Press, 1985.

Whitehead, Andrew L., and Samuel L. Perry. *Taking America Back for God: Christian Nationalism in the United States*. New York: Oxford University Press, 2020.

Zerofsky, Elisabeth. "How the Claremont Institute Became a Nerve Center of the American Right." *New York Times Magazine*, August 3, 2022. https://tinyurl.com/msmbzenc.

——. "The Orbán Effect." *New York Times Magazine*, October 24, 2021, 22–29.

Index

authoritarian reactionary Christian politics
in Brazil, 129–30
characteristics of, 2, 33, 44–53, 82, 95
vs. Christian nationalism, 44, 57
contradictions in, 48, 68, 79
vs. democratic commitment, 183–90
dominant communities in, 160–61
education and, 47–48
in France, 77–79, 81
global trends in, 3, 145
in Hungary, 114, 115
perspectives driving, 33–34
in Poland, 68, 110–12
political ethics and, 80, 111
quasi-Christian religion and, 95
radicalization in, 56, 139–40
revolution/counterrevolution in, 57–58, 60
in Russia, 68, 97–103
strategies of, 34, 139
as threat to democracy, 47–48
in United States (see United States, ARC politics in)
weakened organized religion and, 80, 95
white racism in, 165
Aydin-Düzgit, Senem, 106–7

Bannon, Steve, 80, 122, 130
Baptist democratic tradition
covenant in, 151, 158, 178
democratic church practices, 46–47, 157–60, 162
early democracy and, 154–57
summary of resources from, 184
Baptist World Alliance, 155
Barrès, Maurice, 74, 77, 79
Barreto, Raimundo, 125, 128, 130
Barth, Karl, 92
"Benedict Option," 67
Bible, Christian, 45, 47, 90, 177–78
Bible, Hebrew, 27
Biden, Joseph, 2, 137, 142
Bill of Rights, 14
Black Christian abolitionism, 166–67
Black Christian democratic tradition
democratic commitment in, 168–72, 173–75
resistance in, 166–67
summary of resources from, 184
Black Lives Matter, 137, 138
Black Social Gospel, 166–67
Black Theology of Liberation, A (Cone), 166
blood and soil, 88
Boebert, Lauren, 139
Bolsonaro, Eduardo, 130

lawmaking paradox in, 9
measuring health of, 16–18,
 36, 75
moral approach of, 9–10,
 12–16, 190–91
norms and practices of, 18–20,
 35–36, 159–60
relation to authoritarianism,
 36
vs. republic, 140–42
restoring in United States, 154,
 159–60, 173–75, 181–83
robustness of, 24, 191
temporary triumph of, 29–30
theory of, 12–13
in United States, 70–71
vulnerabilities of, 20–22, 29,
 40, 164
vs. "whiteness," 166–68
democracy, opposition and
 threats to
ARC politics, 47–48
authoritarianism, 30–35, 44
Communism, 28–29
from elite minorities, 21n15
fascism and Nazism, 29
global scope of, 3–4
nationalism, 41
from political right *vs.* left, 6,
 29, 31, 34, 82
radical Islam, 30
religious views driving, 22,
 153, 154

revolution/counterrevolution,
 59–60, 70
three waves of, 23, 50–51, 60,
 61
ultranationalism, 41
weakened norms, 35–36
democracy, representative, 10,
 22, 141
democratic covenantal tradition
in early America, 176, 179–80
restoring in United States,
 181–83
summary of resources from, 185
Demon in Democracy, The (Legutko), 109–10
Deneen, Patrick, 152
despair-utopianism rhetoric, 88
Des réactions politiques (Constant), 49
Deutsche Christen (DC) movement, 92–93
direct democracy, 10, 22, 141–42
disinformation campaigns, 136,
 137
Doerfler, Ryan, 14n10
Doriot, Jacques, 75
Douthat, Ross, 135n4
Dreher, Rod, 67, 119
Dreyfus, Alfred, 76, 77, 78
Drieu La Rochelle, Pierre, 74–75
Du Bois, W. E. B., 167

Eberstadt, Mary, 134n4
economic rights, 156–57

elections
  in Brazil, 126–27
  democratic norms for, 19
  in Hungary, 116–17
  in Poland, 107
  political authoritarianism and,
    35
  rise of Nazism through, 29
  in United States, 136
Elmers, Glenn, 66–67
Embrace of Unreason (Brown),
  72, 74
*End of White Christian America,
  The* (Jones), 165
Enlightenment ideals, 73
Enlightenment liberalism,
  151–52, 153, 154
Erdoğan, Recep Tayyip, 3–4
eschatological politics, 65–66
European Union (EU)
  as advocate for democracy, 30
  Hungary's relations with, 118
  Poland's relations with, 31–32,
    45, 104–5, 113
evangelicalism, 128–30, 138, 139

fascism
  as antithetical to democracy,
    29, 90
  characteristics of, 37, 38–39, 90
  "Christian" versions of, 42
  defined, 37
  in Europe, 29, 74, 75, 77–79
  populism and, 39–41
Fascism: A Warning (Albright), 37

fascist politics, 37–38
fascist state, 37–38
Federalist Papers, 141–42
Feuerbach, Ludwig, 91
Fidesz party, 115
Finchelstein, Federico, 38–39,
  40–41
Flake, Lincoln, 98
France (1870–1944)
  ARC in, 77–79, 81
  culture wars in, 74–76, 79
  Nazi influence in, 76–77
  political alternation in, 73–74
  ultranationalist revival in, 81
Francis (pope), 46
Franco, Marielle, 127
Freedom House, comments of
  on Brazil, 124, 127, 128
  on democratic health mea-
    sures, 16–18, 36
  on Hungary, 115, 116, 118
  on Poland, 104, 106, 107–8
  on Russia, 97
  on United States, 132–33,
    136–38
freedom of speech, 18–19, 35
French, David, 80
French Revolution
  modern democracy and, 28, 73
  political strife following, 49,
    73–74
  as secular revolution, 60–61,
    73, 77, 155
  Vichy regime and, 76–77

INDEX

Kaczyński, Jarosław, 108
Kaczyński, Lech, 109
Kaltwasser, Cristóbal, 39–40
Kasyanov, Mikhail, 100n9
Kazin, Michael, 40
King, Martin Luther, Jr.,
    168–69, 170, 174, 180–81
Kingdom Ethics (Gushee and
    Stassen), 146
Kirill, patriarch, 99–100
Klingenstein, Thomas, 69
Koyzis, David, 8
Kulturkampf, 90

Lagarde, Paul de
    antisemitism of, 89
    Germanic ideology shaped by,
        85, 86–90, 172
    quasi-Christian faith shaped
        by, 91–93, 94
Lake, Kari, 69n6
Lamoreaux, Jeremy, 98
land, relationship to, 68
Langbehn, Julius, 85, 86–90, 94
Laval, Pierre, 75
Law and Justice (PiS) party, 104,
    106, 108, 110–12
Lee, Hak Joon, 177
Legutko, Ryszard
    anti-gay views of, 109–10
    EU criticized by, 31–32, 45, 105
    influence of, 108–9
    pro-authoritarian views of, 45
Leland, John, 155–56

Leontyev, Konstantin, 102
Le Pen, Marine, 81
Letters to Martin (Jelks), 169–70
Levitsky, Steven, 35, 135
LGBTQ+ issues. *See* an-
    ti-LGBTQ+ rhetoric
"liberal," 87
liberal democratic theory, 12–16
liberalism, classical, 153, 154
liberalism, Enlightenment,
    151–52, 153, 154
liberal left, American, 29, 31,
    49, 172–73
libertarian democratic tradition,
    13, 14, 15
Liénart, Cardinal, 79
Locke, John, 12–13
Louis XVI, 73
Louis Philippe I, 74
Lula da Silva, Luiz Inácio, 126
lying, 38

"Make America Great Again," 57
Manif pour tous movement, 81
Marantz, Andrew, 119
Marion, Jean-Luc, 82
Maritain, Jacques, 46n4
Martin, Garret, 120–21
Massachusetts Constitution,
    176, 179–80
Mastriano, Doug, 140
Maurras, Charles, 74, 75, 77, 79,
    80, 81
McGreevy, John, 46n4

right-wing Christian cul-
ture-wars populism, 57
Roe v. Wade, 134, 135n4
Roman Catholicism
  in Brazil, 128-30
  European fascism and, 78
  in France, 77-79, 81
  Kulturkampf against, 90
  natural law in, 9-10
  in Poland, 110-12
  power structures in, 46
  revolution/counterrevolution
    and, 60-61, 73, 77-79, 81
Roman Republic, 141
romantic "idealism," 88
rule of law, 8-9, 19-20, 35
"rule of the people," 11
Russert, Bruce, 8, 148
Russia
  ARC politics in, 68, 97-103
  Orthodox Church support for
    Putin, 96, 97-100, 103, 112
  Putin's regime in, 96-97
  Russkiy mir renewed in,
    100-102
  secular revolution in, 60-61
  Ukraine invasion by, 97,
    99-100, 102-3
Russian Orthodox Church,
  60-61, 96, 97-100, 103, 112
"Russian world" (*Russkiy mir*)
  concept, 100-102

same-sex marriage, 81
Sanders, Ron, 16, 147

SBC (Southern Baptist Conven-
  tion), 159
Second Great Awakening, 70
Second Vatican Council, 46, 79
"secular," 59n2
"secularization," 59n2
settler movement, 64-66
Shortall, Sarah, 46n4
Sikorski, Radoslaw, 108
Snyder, Timothy, 37
socialism, 74
Social-Liberal Party, 124
social unity, 88, 89
Solidarity movement, 106-7
Soros, George, 121
Southern Baptist Convention,
  159
Soviet Union, 30
Stanley, Jason, 37-38, 41
Stassen, Glen
  authoritarianism opposed by,
    160, 161
  on Christianity and democ-
    racy, 147-53, 156
  just peacemaking theory,
    147-48
  minority perspective of, 161
  pro-democracy views of,
    146-47, 148, 157, 160
  on SBC, 159
Stassen, Harold, 146-47
state power, misuse of, 35
Stephens, Bret, 32-33
Stern, Fritz, 84, 85, 86-92, 93,
  94-95